Evangelical Fundamentalists
What They Believe and the Impact They Have

By
Lou Wislocki
Ex-Fundamentalist Pastor

EVANGELICAL FUNDAMENTALISTS
WHAT THEY BELIEVE AND THE IMPACT THEY HAVE

By Lou Wislocki

Second Edition, 2020

First printing: 2019
ISNB: 9781701513273
Papias Press
1121 Veto St NW
Grand Rapids, MI 49504
www.lwislocki@gmail.com

About the Author

Lou graduated from Shelton College, a small fundamentalist school, in 1975, and attended Faith Theological Seminary in Philadelphia. He was elected as pastor to Pilgrim Congregational Church in Metamora, Michigan in 1977, and ordained as a minister in 1979. For twenty-eight years, he pastored three congregations respectively in two states. After resigning from his last congregation, he concluded the Bible is a collection of human religious documents, not the inerrant or infallible *Word of God*. He plans to continue writing about religion, the Bible, and faith from a secular perspective. He resides in Grand Rapids, MI.

Other books by Lou Wislocki:

The Evolution of the Gospel in the Bible

Table of Contents

Preface

Preface

What are evangelical fundamentalists?

Evangelicalism describes a broadly Christian perspective cutting across denominational lines. Its origin can be traced to the Reformation in the sixteenth century or to the Baptist and Mennonite movements of the same period. Evangelicals have a more recent connection to the Great Awakening, an evangelistic crusade in Great Britain and American colonies in the eighteenth century, led by Anglican evangelists George Whitefield and John Wesley, who both preached to large open-air crowds. Though he never preached outside his church, Jonathan Edwards, a New England Congregationalist, is also associated with this group. His best-known sermon, *Sinners in the Hand of an Angry God*, resulted in revivals throughout New England. None of them would have called themselves fundamentalists.

The English word *evangel* is derived from the Greek *euangelion,* which means *good news* and is used extensively throughout the New Testament. The *good news* is summed up by the Apostle Paul in his first letter to the Corinthians: "For I delivered to you first of all that which I also received, how that Christ died for our sins according to the scriptures; and that he was buried, and that he rose again the third day" (15:3,4, KJV).

If you understand evangelicals as Christians who believe in communicating the good news aggressively, you are correct. The drumbeat is that everyone must hear the *good news* about Jesus Christ, and every believer should tell it with a "passion for souls." Why does everyone need to hear the message? So, they may enter into a saving relationship with Jesus Christ by faith. Why is that important? It is the only way anyone may have eternal life. That means when the believer dies, his or her spirit will enter the presence of God, and when Jesus returns, he will raise the believer from the dead and reunite the body with the soul. The believer will be with Christ in heaven forever. Those who do not believe will burn in hell.

Evangelicals today do not believe they are fundamentalists, a pejorative word. It has become more of a description, an adjective. Evangelicals will tell you fundamentalists are religious extremists who tell people in the LGBTQ community they're going to hell. They don't watch movies, drink, vape, or dance, and some handle rattlesnakes. The difference, however, is nuanced. Evangelicals don't tell people they're

5

going to hell directly, but they still believe gays and lesbians who don't repent of their lifestyles will go to hell. I will deal with this subtle difference later.

Fundamentalists can describe believers from any group or religion: Roman Catholics, Jehovah's Witness, Baptists, Muslims, Hindus, Jews, etc. Their common characteristic is an adherence to a strict interpretation of sacred texts or traditions. That does not mean fundamentalists are dangerous; most of them are not. They are dangerous only when they attempt to force their beliefs and practices on the general public. The Salem witch trial in the seventeenth century is an American example. The imposition of Muslim Sharia Law is another example, as found in monarchies like Saudi Arabia and Brunei.

The Emergence of Modernism

Fundamentalism has its origin in the early twentieth century as an evangelical reaction to a hundred years of biblical literary criticism, which originated in Europe and leaped the pond to North America. The objective of scholarly criticism is to examine the Bible as a collection of human literature instead of the inerrant Word of God. The new method of investigation resulted in discovering the first five books of Moses comprise four different oral traditions. While sources originating with Moses may have been passed down orally with each generation, unknown persons wrote them centuries later. However, no compositions in the Hebrew or Christian Bible are exempt from scholarly criticism. Evidence is evidence; for example, the Apostle Paul did not write all the letters ascribed to him. There are many other examples.

Protestant scholars and leaders who accepted the discoveries of biblical criticism were labeled *Christian Modernists*, setting the stage for *fundamentalists versus modernists* controversies in the early twentieth century. For clarification, it may be helpful to think of fundamentalists as religious conservatives and modernists as liberals.

Orthodox and evangelical Christianity was in crisis. Fundamentalist theologians, pastors, and congregations separated from denominations they believed were crumbling to religious modernism. They formed new denominations and vowed to hold onto the conviction that the Bible is the *Word of God*. They remain *staunch* in their traditional beliefs today.

The Fundamentals of the Faith

American and British conservative evangelical theologians and church leaders collaborated in writing 90 essays in a 12-volume encyclopedia entitled *The Fundamentals of the Faith*, published between 1910 and 1915. The battle lines were drawn. *Fundamentalism* was born and with it and the proud title of *Fundamentalist*.

They maintained traditional Christian teachings were fundamental (absolutely necessary) to the Christian faith. Without committing to these essential teachings, one cannot be a Christian. The following are some of the more vital teachings:

1. The Old Testament and the New Testament were written by Prophets and Apostles, who were so inspired by God that what they wrote is the holy and inerrant Word of God.
2. Jesus Christ is the eternal son of God. He is and always was divine, co-equal with God the Father and the Holy Spirit. Jesus Christ is the second person in the Trinity--the Father, the Son, and the Holy Spirit. Jesus rose from the dead and is now seated at the right hand of God.
3. The Son of God became flesh when the virgin Mary conceived him by the power of the Holy Spirit. His mission was to live a holy life, provide his disciples with new instructions and to suffer and die on the cross as a sacrifice for all people to cleanse them of all sin, making them acceptable to God the Father.
4. Upon death, the souls of believers will be with God until the time Jesus returns. He will raise the dead. He will reunite their souls with their bodies, and so they will forever be with the Lord. Unbelievers upon death go to hell.

While variations exist across the spectrum of theologies, the teachings listed above are also doctrines of the Christian Church historically (Roman Catholic, Orthodox, and Protestant), and they are embraced by evangelicals today.

Many, if not most evangelicals, are fundamentalists. Of course, any person or group can reject a title or repudiate a doctrine. A distinct characteristic of evangelicals is avid proselytism, a practice they refer to as "soul-winning." Today you may hear of it as "presenting Christ" or sharing "God's love."

Billy Graham

One of the greatest icons of evangelical fundamentalism until his death in 2018 was the Rev. Billy Graham, who maintained throughout the twentieth century the revivalists preaching style of Dwight L. Moody (b.1837, d.1899) and Billy Sunday (b.1862, d.1932). Graham believed in angels, demons, and hell as the destination of unrepentant sinners.

Graham was a great orator whose delivery was passionate, compelling, and convincing. His oratory was flawless. He could keep the listener hanging on every word and eager for more. I no longer agree with the message of Billy Graham. To his credit, Graham detested racial segregation and avoided taking political sides.

God and Politics

God and politics have been strange bedfellows for 100 years, perhaps from the very beginning of North America having been settled by Puritans fleeing persecution in England. New Englanders were staunch Calvinists who viewed themselves as establishing a new theocracy, a nation governed by the principles of the Bible. As late as 1820, thirty-one years after the ratification of the Constitution of the United States, many towns in Massachusetts, using a Sabbath gate, prevented travelers from passing through on the Lord's Day.[1] Many fundamentalists will argue the Founding Fathers intended for the United States to be a Christian nation. While the Constitution prevents a national religion, I believed many, perhaps most, leaders in the early republic assumed the United States would always be Christian. They could not imagine that it would be anything else.

The Scopes Monkey Trial

In 1925 the Tennessee legislature passed the Butler Act, which prohibited public school teachers in the state from denying the biblical account of creation, effectively preventing the teaching of the biological evolution of human beings. Governor Austin Peay signed the Act into law the same year.

The ACLU (American Civil Liberties Union) challenged the new law when John Scopes, a public-school teacher, was fined $100 to $500 for each offense of teaching evolution. While the trial occurred in the small town of Dayton, it drew national and global attention. William

---

[1] Josiah Quincy, *Figures of the Past* (New York: Little, Brown and Company, 1883), 25.

Jennings Bryant, the well-known, three-time Democratic nominee for president and Secretary of State for Woodrow Willow, participated in the trial, supporting the State's prosecution. Bryant was also a fundamentalist who defended the divine inspiration of the Bible. While he denied evolution, he affirmed the evangelical compromised of the *Long Day Theory of Creation*, which interpreted the days of creation as indefinite periods of time.[2]

The famous lawyer and agnostic, Clarence Darrow, defended Scopes. Many major newspapers in the United States covered the trial. The prosecution won its case. Upon appeal by the defense, the Tennessee Supreme Court upheld the original court's decision. The Butler Act remained in force until the legislature repealed it in 1967.

The Republican and Democratic parties reversed roles in the 1930s. In the 19th century, Republicans represented northern and liberal interests while Democrats represented southern and conservative interests and values. Today, it is the opposite.

The Scopes trial revealed how the controversy between fundamentalists and modernists deeply affected society and politics and for how long. Evangelical fundamentalists have allied with political conservatives, while Christian modernists have allied with political liberals. The political and religious divide has shifted from North versus South to urban versus rural. Democrats and Republicans today barely resemble the political parties they were in Lincoln's day.

The Faith Advisory Committee

President Trump created a *Faith Advisory Committee* that includes many prominent fundamentalists and evangelical leaders who openly support the President as a god-send to champion their causes, among them, an end to legalized abortion by stacking the Supreme Court of the United States with judges who might overturn Roe vs. Wade. Members of the Committee include evangelical fundamentalist leaders Jerry Falwell Jr., James Dobson, and other notable preachers and evangelists. Dobson founded Focus on the Family, a non-profit organization promoting fundamentalist values through his radio program and other media outlets. He has endorsed *gay conversion therapy* as a

---

[2]"Butler Act," Wikipedia, last modified August 4, 2019, http://wikipedia.org/wiki/Bulter_Act.

legitimate treatment to cure men and women of their gay and lesbian lifestyles. He officially supported Donald Trump for the presidential election in 2016.

Jerry Falwell (b.1933, d.2007) was a fundamentalist, televangelist, and conservative activist who founded Liberty University in 1971 to educate evangelical fundamentalist leaders. Falwell also founded *The Moral Majority*, a lobbying organization to promote Christian-Conservative causes and Republican candidates for political office. In 1980, *The Moral Majority* chose Ronald Reagan as their candidate for President of the United States. Jerry Falwell Jr. succeeded his father as President of Liberty University and invited then-candidate Donald Trump to speak at the university on January 18, 2016. President Trump also delivered the commencement address at Liberty on May 13, 2017.

President Donald Trump continues to play to the evangelical fundamentalist community for their support for the 2020 election. The marriage between evangelical fundamentalism to the conservative Republican Party is sealed and unmistakable.

Not all evangelicals are politically liberal. In the 1970s, some evangelicals recognized the dangerous coupling of fundamentalism with the republican party. They have attempted to separate politics from religion and express a social conscience to acknowledge the "plight of many who are poor, vulnerable, or without a voice in their communities."[3] However, they believe the same evangelical fundamentalist teachings listed above, except they omit any reference to hell. I will cover more about their position in Chapter 15, *The Conflict with Science*.

What Follows

While evangelical fundamentalism is only one component negatively affecting and dividing American society, it is dominant. It is the sub-culture I understand well. Not only are they committed to ending abortion in all circumstances, but they also regard the rights of the LGBTQ community as destroying the moral fabric of society. Evangelical fundamentalism is a corrosive social and political element in modern society.

---

[3] Evangelical Manifesto, May 7, 2008, evangelicalmanifesto.com

Evangelical fundamentalists and their beliefs are described, showing how those beliefs are derived from the books of the Bible and Christian tradition. While I am no longer a Christian—I do not see or feel the need—I believe Modernist Christians, with their emphasis on tolerance, are a positive moral force in America. Tolerance is not their only virtue; compromise also has been significant.

The problem is people believing in the Bible as the inerrant Word of God. The Bible contains myths, historical inaccuracies, and contradictions. It is not a natural science textbook, though fundamentalist evangelicals use it that way—Adam and Eve, the global flood, every species of insect and animal gathered into the ark, Moses parting the Red Sea, etc. Books and letters of the Bible were ascribed to people who didn't write them and compiled by people about whom we know nothing.

Does the Bible have any value? Of course, it does, as human literature. Adventure and romantic novellas, poetry, history, wisdom literature, and more are found in its pages. Bible stories contain valuable lessons, as do the parables of Jesus. Greek Mythology offers as much; however, it is not God's authoritative message to human beings?

But neither the Bible nor any so-called sacred text is the *Word of God*. All religious texts have their value, providing moral lessons, stories, histories, beliefs, fears, hopes, and worldviews of the cultures that produced them. Those cultures were not only separated geographically, but historically. There is little resemblance between the religion of King David's Israel and the Judaism of Jesus' Palestine. Religion evolves constantly.

I relate my own experience becoming an evangelical fundamentalist, my time as a pastor, and my ministry to members of the congregations I served. While some of my recorded experiences and dialogues are humorous or awkward, they are intended to show what evangelicals believe and why, why some beliefs are positive and why others are negative and harmful.

I conclude the book with my resignation from the Christian ministry and my departure from the faith. It was a journey that lasted 41 years.

While names of locations and institutions are real, the names of private persons are changed to protect their right to privacy. I have retained the names of persons well known from media exposure and publications.

11

I have used the King James Version, also known as the Authorized Version, and have updated older English words when quoting. Some verses are my translation.

Abbreviations for other translations used:

ESV—English Standard Version

MINE—My translation or paraphrase

NIV—New International Version

RSV—Revised Standard Version

TNIV—Today's New International Version

Chapter 1

The Beginning:

In and Out of Faith and Back Again

I grew up in a somewhat Christian home. My parents were what evangelicals today would call *nominal* Christians—in name only. Yes, they took us to church, and we had a family Bible containing fascinating color illustrations of God creating Adam, Abraham with a knife raised to sacrifice Isaac, Jacob wrestling with God, Moses parting the Red Sea, and, of course, Jesus healing the sick. I would flip through to the pictures with interest then set it back on top of the secretary desk in front of the mirror where it collected dust. My parents didn't read it. We never prayed before meals, but I am sure that if someone asked my parents what faith they were, they would undoubtedly have said, "Christian," without the least hesitation.

My dad grew up Polish-Catholic and attended parochial school. My mom was from an Irish-Polish home that was Baptist. They decided a good compromise was to become Episcopalian.

We attended church in Hammond, about a half-hour drive from Cedar Lake, Indiana. For a while, we attended every Sunday. It was there I was first exposed to Sunday school—flannel board figures and metal folding chairs, kid-size. Our Sunday-school teacher led us downstairs to a room with clean, shiny tile floors smelling of lemon-scented wax, with white insulated ceiling panels, and windows just below the ceiling—a scene familiar to millions of kids in North America. Some church basements clean and shiny, others scuffed and a little dirty with steel posts rusting at the base.

She got us in the right mood with a few easy kid songs. I remember the song, "He's got the whole world in his hands." There were a lot of hand motions to represent the whole world, the place where God lives, hands put together to form a bowl--God's hands. I think the song was more of a hit in modernist churches. The flannel figures of children—yellow, black, and white—connected by their cuffs: *regardless of color, we are connected, one human family*. What did the song and flannel board represent? Security, protection, love, acceptance, the positive power of God. African and Asian kids were our brothers and

13

sisters. We didn't have any in our church. But it was a positive message for little kids who would become adults.

However, it was also a false interpretation of reality. The year was 1958. Black adults and children were suffering from injustice and poverty throughout the United States. I was a little white kid who was blissfully ignorant. God's eyes are not on every sparrow, nor does he hold the whole world in his hands. Either that, or he's not doing a good job.

Mom and Dad found out about a new Episcopal church getting started in Crown Point, 15 minutes closer to home, so we started going there. The would-be congregation rented an older church edifice the Methodists had vacated when they built a new church a few blocks down—the same one in which I would officiate my brother's wedding many years later. The old church was a temporary site. Plans were underway to build a new one further out of town and even closer to home.

We stopped attending the Episcopal Church because my parents decided to enroll my two older sisters and me in the parochial school, which meant that we had to become Catholic. They thought we would get a better education there, and we did. Conversion meant rebaptism for all of us. My siblings and I attended Mass every school day with our classmates at 8 AM. In a few years, I became an acolyte (*altar boy*) and quite often assisted in the 5:45 AM Mass. The nuns and about four older women were usually in attendance. Mom was a trooper; she dropped me off in the morning and picked me up at 6:30. Then it was back to Mass at 8 o'clock with everyone else. I quit when the Mass was changed to English—all that work memorizing Latin responses went down the tubes.

The education was excellent, and the discipline consistent. The priest visited class once a month during catechism hour. He would ask random questions for anyone to answer. He once posed a hypothetical question: "If you were stranded on a deserted island as a small child and no adults survived, and you never heard about God, would you grow up to believe in God?" The room was silent as he looked around for someone to raise a hand.

I was thinking, imagining the scenario. I raised my hand, and he called on me. "Yes," I said with certainty. All eyes looked at me.

He was pleased. "Very good, you're right, but why?"

14

"Well," I said, "I would look up at the sun, moon, and stars and believe that someone made them, and that would be God."

"Thank you. That's exactly right." I scored. He then went on to explain the existence of God from the design of creation, an argument as old as philosophy. It is right to the extent that ancient people did that; they didn't have modern science to explain the world. Without an education, I would have grown up on the Island, believing the sun revolved around the earth, wondering and imagining.

When I entered the fifth grade, I began to think.

I learned all the usual subjects—multiplication and division, how to diagram a sentence, spelling, how to write dictation, geography, and history, especially church history. We also learned a little Roman history from a book written on our level. I remember the drawings. The lessons involved the historical context in which Christ was born, his crucifixion, and the saints' martyrdom. When everyone around you, everyone at school, and in your family believes in the Father, the Son, and the Holy Spirit, it's impossible not to believe. It is part of what I will deal with in more detail as the *collective imagination,* a strange tribal psychology that gets people to believe what the tribe believes. Who doesn't want to be part of the tribe?

I learned about heaven, purgatory, hell, and how to get into the first place and avoid the other two, but it looked more likely that most of us were going to have a spend time in purgatory, a place where the fire burned as hot as hell.

My hand went up. Sister acknowledged. "How long could I be in purgatory?

"It will be different for everyone," she replied. "One year, maybe a thousand or more."

I tried to imagine burning for 1,000 years. The image is stuck in my head forever—a kind of pre-purgatory.

There were ways to avoid it: going to confession and finishing your penance on the rosary (I still think rosaries are beautiful little works of art) and wearing the right collection of religious medals in the event you died accidentally, *which you never know could always happen.* One had to remain vigilant. However, escaping purgatory seemed futile anyway because only bona fide saints went straight to heaven. I tried rosaries and medals for a while but quickly tired of them. Ultimately, that's what can happen with religion. You get tired of it.

There was the teaching about the Holy Trinity, the great mystery we had to believe even if we couldn't understand it. There was the story of a great church father who walked the beach deep in thought, trying to understand the Trinity. He saw a child digging a hole in the sand, trying to fill it with the sea using a small bucket.

"What are you doing?" he asked the child.

"I'm going to fill this hole with all the water in the sea."

The church father laughed. "You'll never be able to fill that hole with the sea."

"Nor will you ever be able to understand the Trinity," the child said and disappeared. The child was an angel, you see, with a message from God.

There was the story of the 50 Protestant men who met every morning to pray for Catholics to become Protestant. One day, while in prayer, they were miraculously converted to Catholicism, and from that day on, they prayed for Protestants to become Catholics.

Catholics had lots of stories like that.

Leaving the Faith

My parents—when you're a minor, it always begins with your parents—were helping to organize a high school in Cedar Lake. For years, after graduation from 8th grade, kids were bused either to Crown Point or Lowell high schools. I don't understand how things were done then or now to organize a school, but the important thing is, they did everything they were required to do and succeeded.

"How would you kids like to attend the new junior high and high school?" My parents asked us.

It appealed to my older sister and me. Two younger siblings didn't get asked. They would attend the Jane Ball elementary school.

The new school was exciting and fun. I played basketball and always made the starting lineup. Many of the teachers were young graduates from universities in our state, enthusiastic about teaching. The most exciting thing was exposure to a secular understanding of the world.

16

I knew of only one teacher who cautiously admitted to a few students he was an evangelical Christian. He was an excellent English teacher. His father was a retired evangelical pastor. Later, the teacher converted to Catholicism to the chagrin of his parents. Other teachers who may have been Christian kept it to themselves. Students also hid their faith. My best friend was an evangelical and never mentioned it. The hottest girl in my class was a Baptist, but you would have never guessed it. So yes, it was a godless school, and it was great.

Attending a public school was all about learning without God, learning about the world and its history, and the living and nonliving things in it that you could research, feel or see in a microscope. It was attending sports events and dances, seeing which girl might be there. In 7th grade, we read *Gulliver's Travels* and then discussed what Jonathan Swift was satirically saying about English society and government in his own time, eighteenth-century England. I loved it. The *Red Badge of Courage* by Stephen Crane was the next reading. My English teacher inspired me to enjoy literature and writing.

I forgot about God and never missed him. The family stopped attending church for about two years, and then my parents got it in their heads that we should return to church. The Episcopal Church had its new building halfway to Cedar Lake from Crown Point. One Sunday morning, they said, "Get dressed, we're going to church." I protested vehemently but futilely. I submitted, but not without ranting. The worship service was okay. Sweet donuts and coffee after service made it better.

The pastor did what a good pastor should do. He made an appointment to visit our family after dinner. My parents told us we could participate if we wanted to. I was the only one who joined in. I forget his name, but he was a nice enough middle-aged, slightly overweight man with a gentle and humorous disposition. We sat around the small coffee table in the living room with cups of coffee or tea. I listened, and after a while, he asked me if I had any questions. I did, but I can't remember what they were. I was sincere and polite; he appreciated my questions and answered them intelligently.

Our stint in the church didn't last very long. My parents were very conservative; however, in their opinion, the Episcopal Church had become more liberal politically. The African American community was struggling against segregation and for equal rights. My parents were suspicious of black activist leaders. Racist propaganda circulated that some of them were communists. In the mid-60s, that was the worst kind of person you could be, a *commie*. Whites in all-white communities like ours didn't understand or didn't want to understand what blacks were upset about. There were no blacks in Cedar Lake.

"They used to be so quiet and peaceful. We never had any trouble from them before," my mother would say. Many people in the North closed their eyes to the reality of racism. To that extent, they were racists.

When whites saw police officers on T.V. abusing peaceful black protesters, they blamed it on the protestors for being troublemakers. My parents didn't like protesters, white or black; they were ungrateful and seditious long-haired hippies. The nation was also bitterly divided over Vietnam. People were convinced of the *domino theory*—if Vietnam fell to communism, what country would fall next?

As soon as my mother saw a poster in the church supporting Angela Davis, a famous female black leader, that was it. The church had grown a social conscience. Mom had not, so we left the church. A female member of the church called mom to find out what happened. Mom gave her an earful about communists.

Radio Christian

Not long after, she wanted to return to her Baptist roots. Her sister had a born-again experience and began working on my mother. Mom also started listening to the Rev. Carl McIntire on the radio. He was a fundamentalist and ultra-conservative rabble-rouser who merged political conservatism with fundamentalism—a trend that persists today. McIntire built a nonprofit organization which included a newspaper called the *Christian Beacon* and a syndicated radio program, *The Twentieth Century Reformation Hour,* which aired on Christian radio stations across the U.S. and Canada. He railed against the World Council of Churches as a modernist organization no longer faithful to Christ or the Bible as the Word of God. The pastor of Collingswood Bible Presbyterian Church, he became and remained the dominant leader of the Bible Presbyterian Church (Denomination) until losing control in the 1980s and subsequently leading his congregation out of the group.

In 1965, McIntire became the President of Shelton College, a small non-denominational evangelical school in Ringwood, New Jersey. The school moved to Cape May, New Jersey, in 1963. He moved the college to Cape Canaveral, Florida, in 1971 because the New Jersey State

Board of Education determined the college could no longer grant degrees. In 1971 he hired Hyland Shephard as the President and appointed himself Chancellor in 1973 to maintain control. The college moved back to Cape May in 1979. It closed in 1992.

Mom became a born-again believer quietly but talked to us about our need to be born again. No longer a nominal believer, she became a radio-Christian. Mom was the emotional one; my Aunt was the logical one with the ability to debate effectively with her nieces and nephews.

Back in the Saddle Again

While this was going on, I was able to escape into humanism—my books and attempts at writing short stories. We lived in the largest apartment in a big two-story building. We moved into it after my father closed the tavern on the ground floor and converted it into half of our living space, including my parents' bedroom. We kids occupied five bedrooms upstairs. There were three other apartments—one upstairs and two down. We were able to seclude ourselves in our rooms, far from the madding crowd. It was a unique upbringing.

I finished high school a semester early and remained at home while I waited for a call to work on an ore carrier on the Great Lakes, another story. There was nothing to do in the winter but read and write. Along with idleness, I developed a habit for listening—out of mom's sight—to Rev. McIntire's broadcasts, which aired daily, weekdays, for a half-hour. He was a skilled rhetorician and orator, a dangerous combo. I found myself inclining to his rational conservatism and irrational fundamentalism. At the same time, I began pondering the meaning of life—a risky path. Mostly, I was feeling lost and anxious about my future; I didn't know what to do with my life or where to go.

There was another lingering influence. Two years before, I began reading *War and Peace*, a birthday gift from my parents. I was not only impressed with Tolstoy's ability as a great novelist; he was an intellectual with a vast knowledge of history, philosophy, and politics. Throughout the novel, he breaks into reflections on the science of history, mathematics, and philosophy. He was also a Christian—howbeit, liberal. I realized a Christian could be an intellectual. Read theology books, and you'll understand. The exposure to Tolstoy slumbered in the recesses of my mind.

While I was waiting for employment in the spring as an Ordinary Seaman on the Lakes, an Army recruiter convinced me to take the Army physical and written exam in Chicago. There was no commitment to enlist. Army recruiters are slick and know what they're doing. I met an older schoolmate there who had dropped out of school and was "re-upping." He expected to go back to Vietnam. Years ago, he beat me up at the bus stop, and I had to cry "uncle" to get out of his chokehold. The fight was my fault; I had challenged him. When we reconnected at the exam center, we were at peace. We chatted. I mostly listened.

I chose not to enlist then. I wasn't afraid of going to Nam; the war was winding down. I wanted to attend college but hadn't decided where to attend. Being lost, I was ripe for conversion. I wanted direction. I was already reading the Synoptic Gospels in the New Testament.

On April 9, 1971, I became a born-again Christian.

In a moment of epiphany, I knelt on the ground beneath the trees, looking at the cumulus clouds drifting by on a warmer than usual spring day. As a fundamentalist writer had instructed, I closed my eyes and asked the Holy Spirit to come into my heart. It happened. I felt it—the love of God and the control of God over my life. I felt peace and joy. When I opened my eyes, the world looked different. I saw God in everything. I came to a new realization of who and what I was and what I had to do. You can't question a person's experience, even if you think it imagined. Feelings and emotions are real. I told Mom, who was ecstatic.

The next day, I got a call from *Lake Carriers Hall* informing me an ore boat needed a deckhand. That afternoon, dad drove me to the docks in south Chicago. Before we left, Mom presented me with a small Bible. I kept it for over 40 years until it began to fall apart.

Onward Christian Soldier

In early July, I disembarked the ship in Cleveland and called home. Mom answered, and I asked her if someone could pick me up at Greyhound station in Gary. She would. I departed Cleveland the next day.

I faced the problem of my future once again. I decided to enroll in classes at Purdue University Northwest, the Hammond Campus. The university had accepted me earlier that year, but I hadn't followed through. Because it was late enrollment at the end of August, my academic advisor sharply chided me. I recall it was in the basement of a building on campus, and there were a lot of other kids doing the same. I wanted a major in journalism. He put me in three classes that still had vacancies. I wasn't happy with any of them because they weren't even part of the core curriculum. Feeling frustrated, I stuffed the papers in the waste can and walked out. An impulsive decision made within a few seconds changed my life.

"I'm going to call the recruiter and enlist," I told my parents.

Dad was upset and objected. He fought in World War II and didn't want me to go to Vietnam, but mom had a card up her sleeve. Weeks before I boarded the ship last spring, she coaxed me into applying for admission to Shelton College. I complied to get her off my back.

"What about Shelton College? You were accepted there," she reminded me. She always wanted me to attend there. She had been listing to McIntire talk every day about the College moving to Florida. He had transformed the college's exodus from New Jersey from being a mistake into a righteous cause and a testimony to Jesus Christ.

I was not so enthused. My interest in McIntire and his cause had waned. At that moment, I was less excited about my four-month-old faith.

"Yes," my dad jumped in, "Go to Shelton." He hadn't wanted me to go there, but he didn't like the alternative.

"I'll call and see if they'll still take you," she said.

I felt paralyzed and responded feebly, "Okay."

She did. They would still take me. Shelton was a very small college; the administration was in desperate need of students. They accepted everyone.

Like a deer caught in headlights, I stared at the fork in the road of my future. I made the decision that would profoundly determine the course of my life.

Two days later, I was on a flight to Orlando, Florida.

Attending Shelton college transformed me into a thoroughgoing fundamentalist. I became zealous about my faith and the Bible; I wanted to convert everyone. In my junior year, I took the required class, "Philosophy of the Christian Faith." Our textbook was *Systematic*

Theology by Louis Berkhof, a leading Reformed theologian of the early twentieth century who taught at Calvin Theological Seminary in Grand Rapids.

I was hooked. In my senior year, I heard "God's call" to the ministry (it wasn't audible) and later attended Faith Theological Seminary and then Reformation Seminary (a mistake—it and the decision). I went on from there to become a pastor in 1977.

Chapter 2

What Our Ancient Ancestors Believed

That Some Believe Today

"As soon as man became distinguished from the animal, he became religious; that is to say, he saw in Nature something beyond the phenomena, and for himself something beyond death."

Ernest Renan, 1863.[4]

Renan believed when we emerged as homo sapiens, we "saw in Nature something beyond the phenomena," and for ourselves, "something beyond death." The priest in parochial school was right. A person left alone on a deserted Island from infancy would grow up believing in power or powers, god or gods, beyond our world, even if that power was the sun, as the ancient Egyptians believed. Why not? The sun-god, Ra, made everything grow and brought light and warmth to the earth every day.

Three thousand years ago, humans didn't have modern science to help them understand the world in which they lived. Meteorology didn't exist as a science. They must have wondered what is beyond the clouds. Is that where the gods live? Why did one year bring draught while another brought a flood? Why did plagues kill the young and elderly? They reasoned beings greater than humans must be in the world. They are invisible but can appear in various forms—even as humans. Somehow the gods lived above the clouds, maybe with the stars, in the great unknown where humans cannot go. Gods were in the depths of the sea and in the thunder. They sent rain to make crops grow and to quench thirst.

For the ancients, the activities of the gods helped them to understand the world in which they lived. Belief in the supernatural was their interpretation of reality. The gods were involved in their daily lives and appeared to them in different forms (anthropomorphisms). God walked in the Garden of Eden to check on Adam and Eve. They

---

[4] Earnest Renan, "Preface to the Second Edition," in *The Life of Jesus*, 1863.

converted and interacted with God as though it were an ordinary daily activity. Yahweh appeared to Abraham as three men whom he invited to sit and eat with him in his tent on the plains of Mamre (Gen. 18). On his journey back to Canaan, Jacob wrestled with God. He would not let go of God until he received a blessing from him (Gen. 32).

Baal, the god of the Phoenicians and Canaanites, was in the thunder and brought the rain. His wife, Asherah, was the goddess of fertility whose blessing helped female humans and livestock conceive and give birth. Asherah poles dotted the pastures where livestock grazed. Even after the Hebrews began worshipping the Midianite god, some regarded Asherah as his wife. Gods and goddesses were the products of human imagination. They helped to explain what happened in the world and why it happened.

The Savior Motif

Some humans, both men and women alike, were so great, strong, and courageous. They were considered the sons and daughters of the gods by natural insemination and conception. The gods and goddesses came down from heaven, took human forms, and copulated with chosen people.

Goddesses gave birth to sons and daughters who were half-human and half-divine. Some women were "blessed" by the visit of a male god who raped them. They bore half-divine sons and daughters. Heracles (the Roman *Hercules*) was the son of Zeus by a mortal woman, Alcmene. Disguised as her husband, Zeus, raped her. He had many half-divine children. Hera, the goddess-wife of Zeus, persecuted the offspring of his infidelities. Heracles was one of them, known for his extraordinary strength and courage. He destroyed the monsters that preyed on mortals. Upon his death, he became fully divine.

Melqart, the son of the god, Baal Hammon, was the counterpart of Heracles. Originating in the Phoenician city of Tyre, merchants and mercenaries carried the religion of Baal and Melqart to colonies in Sicily, North Africa, and Spain, of which the most famous was the city of Carthage. Statues of both gods appeared together in the Greek and Phoenician settlements of Sicily and Sardinia.[5]

---

[5] Richard Miles, "Chapter 3, The Realm of Heracles-Mel art: Greeks and Carthaginians in the Central Mediterranean," in *Carthage Must be Destroyed* (New York: Viking, a Penguin Group), e-book.

Legends like Heracles and Melqart likely predate history and could be tens of thousands of years old. Heroes were the strong men, the saviors of the tribe from bandits, demons, and monsters. The rulers of tribes were declared sons of God, probably by the rulers themselves or at their behest. The hero-chieftain established himself as the savior of the people. He alone would lead them to security and peace.

In Sumerian mythology, the story of Gilgamesh is older than the Greek myth of Heracles. He was the greatest and strongest king—two-thirds divine and one-third human. His mother was Ninsun, the wise old cow, and his father was Anu, chief among the gods.

We can recognize the Hebrew Sampson as a Heracles figure, with the difference that he was not a son of God in the Greek sense. While Sampson may have lived, storytellers exaggerated his deeds. He did not kill 1,000 Philistines with a donkey's jawbone (Judges 15:14-16). Can you even imagine how that would have played out? Did he create a hill of slain Philistines at his feet while he climbed them?

The Hebrew storytellers added a new twist to the hero-savior epic. God gave Samson superhuman strength. When Delilah cut his long hair—the secret of his strength—and cried out for the last time, "the Philistines are upon you Samson," he rose as before and thought he would "shake himself free, but Yahweh had left him." The Philistines bound him with cords, gouged out his eyes, put him in shackles, and forced him to grind wheat. We can imagine him doing the work of an ox, pushing in a circle the wooden beam of the heavy millstone.

After many days his hair grew back. No one noticed. When the Philistines celebrated in the temple of Dagon, they brought Samson there for entertainment. He asked to be led to the pillars of the temple to support himself. He prayed and asked Yahweh to give him the strength to avenge himself on the Philistines for the loss of his eyes. Yahweh granted his petition. Samson felt each pillar while he was between them and pushed with all his might until the pillars collapsed, and the temple came crashing down, crushing to death all the lords of the Philistines and Samson. He gave his own life and thus saved Israel (Judges 16). Here we have the hero-savior who sacrificed his life for the nation, setting the stage for the suffering servant of Isaiah 53, who must suffer to save all Israel.

The ultimate Jewish hero was the righteous messiah-king who would deliver Israel from all her enemies through wisdom and military prowess. *Messiah* means the *anointed one*, chosen by God to serve him and his people. King David and his son, Solomon, were God's messiahs. The prophet wrote: "This is what the LORD (Yahweh) says to his *anointed* [his *messiah*], to Cyrus 'whose right hand I take hold of...' (Is. 45:1, TNIV). Cyrus was the king of the Medes and Persians who set free the Jewish captives of Babylon in 539 BCE. He was not a convert to Judaism. In Jesus' time, the Jews were anticipating the birth of a descendant of David, who would assume the throne and defeat in battle the Romans and the Herodians.

Appeasing the Gods with Sacrifice

When drought devastated the crops or when marauders invaded the land stealing livestock, it meant the gods were displeased. How could the people appease them? They offered the gods their most valued possession. For a predominantly agrarian society, the offerings were livestock and grain. When and how did priests emerge as the ones who alone could offer sacrifices for the people? We don't know. The priesthood is one of those professions among the most ancient. The priests received their portion for consumption, burnt the inedible parts, and sold what they didn't consume at the market. The Books of Judges and I and II Samuel have ordinary people offering sacrifices at community meals. Samuel blessed the town community meal, identified as a sacrifice (1 Sam. 9:12).

By the time of Solomon, priests increasingly controlled the sole right to offer sacrifices and restrict the practice to the temple. For the ablution of sins, they slaughtered the animals, drained the blood, and sprinkled it on the altar. After the priest took their portion, they distributed the rest to the marketplace. This practice also applied to grain offerings; consequently, the priest had both provision and income. According to the Law, the people were expected to bring a tenth of their produce and livestock to the temple as offerings. As coinage developed, the priest commanded the payment of temple taxes (Exodus 30:11-16).[6] The priests became wealthy food distributors and financiers in Israel.

Throughout the Mediterranean world and until the late seventh century BCE, parents offered their children as burnt sacrifices to Moloch and other gods. Elohim commanded Abraham to sacrifice his only son,

---

[6] This passage of the Torah belongs to a written source that dates no earlier than the 8th century BCE.

Isaac, who was the thing most precious to him. However, Elohim provided a ram caught in the thicket to be a substitute in place of Isaac. Abraham proved his faith, and Elohim was pleased. To their credit, the prophets of Israel strongly condemned child sacrifice and lamented the practice.

Not Much Has Changed?

Evangelical fundamentalists regard the stories of the Bible, the words of the prophets, apostles, and Jesus as the inspired and inerrant Word of God, providing an interpretation of reality. They believe everything written in it is true—historically, spiritually, and scientifically. Thousands of evangelical preachers across America embrace the same biblical interpretation of reality. They believe people do bad things because they are inherently evil. God created Adam and Eve on the same day. They became sinful because they ate the forbidden fruit (Gen. 3). All human beings have inherited Adam's guilt and sinful nature (Rom. 5). The only way God can forgive peoples' sins is by blood sacrifice to appease his anger. In the Christian scheme, God offered what was most precious to him, his divine son, Jesus Christ, who shed his blood for the forgiveness of our sins (Rom. 3:25). However, Jesus had to be willing to give his life as a blood offering (Jn. 10:18).

Jesus Christ and the devil are at war for the souls of people. At times, the devil seems to be winning. In the Book of Revelation, Satan almost succeeds in destroying the children of God before Jesus returns for the rescue. In the meantime, invisible spiritual conflict and competition rage for the eternal souls of human beings.

All these things they believe are factual and true because they are stated in the Bible—the divinely inspired, inerrant, and infallible Word of God.

Evangelical Decline

Fortunately, the number of white evangelicals in America has declined, as some polling figures and analysis show—from 23 percent in 2007 to 17 percent in 2016.[7] However, within that period, the impact of white evangelicalism on social-issues politics is significant. Evangelicals

---

[7] Winston, Kimberly, *Christian America Dwindling, including white evangelicals study shows..*, Religious News Service (blog), September 6,2017, religionnews.com/2017/09/06/embargoed-christian-america-dwindling-including-white-evangelicals-study-shows/

comprise about 35% of the Republican Party. Christians, including all denominations and ethnicities, comprise about 50% of the U.S. population.[8] Religion as an ideology is conservative, clinging to the values and norms of the past. New irreligious ideas are antagonistic to the old, "the tried and true"—the idea and the feeling people trust most. The sentiment has nothing to do with the head but everything to do with the gut. Donald Trump appealed to the gut of religious and conservative Americans.

Protestants include many evangelical fundamentalists and modernists. Baptist and independents, while evangelical, do not consider themselves to be Protestant. Not all Protestants regard the Bible as the inerrant Word of God; many are politically liberal.

President Trump's approval is about 60% among highly religious whites. Fundamentalist evangelicals and conservative Roman Catholics played a significant role in electing Donald Trump as President of the United States. Without their support, he wouldn't have been elected. Many political pundits point to Trump's choice of Mike Pence, an evangelical fundamentalist, to garner the support of that community. The religious divide in the early twenty-first century between the religious and non-religious is one factor behind the political divide between conservatives and progressives.

I live in a mostly white, evangelical, and conservative-Catholic region of the country. It is also very Republican.[9] My experience with white evangelical fundamentalists is that they view reality with a kind of cognitive dissonance (mental discord). They function daily with a scientific and rational understanding of the modern world, while their interpretations and applications of the Bible are non-intellectual and superstitious, as antiquated as the worldview described earlier. Conflicting perceptions of reality exist within the same mind. Interactions in a secular society and marketplace are practical and, therefore, necessarily mundane. However, they combine political loyalties with religious convictions, and the combination is emotional and irrational.

---

[8] Ibid.

[9] However, the situation is changing with shifting demographics. In the 2020 Presidential election, Kent County voted for Joe Biden, giving him 52% of the vote to Trump's 46%. The City of Grand Rapids gave Joe Biden a whapping 70% of the vote. Biden also won decisively in Kalamazoo County.

Many Christian business owners attempt to bridge the dissonance by identifying their businesses as *Christian*. You can find an online Christian Business directory featuring every kind of Christian business in the zip code where you reside. They have an eight-point list of Christian beliefs to which business owners must subscribe to participate.[10] They are identical to the fundamentalist-evangelical teachings I listed in the *Preface*.

A Christian businessperson may call his or her business a Christian business. However, what does that mean? Does it mean she and her employees are more honest? Does being Christian make them somehow better. In Chapter 9, I deal with the spiritual dichotomy of *the saved and the lost*, the other.

A Christian business may begin the day with a prayer meeting but proceeds to operate its business like any of its competitors with the same standards of fairness. Any business, regardless of the faith or lack of faith of its employees, must operate with integrity, or it will eventually fail, or its owner and employees will be prosecuted.

Ethics is secular. As an insurance salesperson, I am required to take and pass a state-approved ethics course every two years. The course is secular; it doesn't contain any religious references.

---

[10] Local Christian Businesses, www.christianpages.com/index.php. Go to "About Us" then "We Believe.

Chapter 3

Why People Believe in God

To find someone in America who doesn't know anything about Jesus would be tough. If you ever encountered someone who said, "I don't know anything about him," it's more likely because they haven't thought about him in a long time. Just ask anyone a question like, "Who was Jesus"? If that person takes the time to talk to you, he or she will probably tell you something accurate about Jesus. That individual might say, "he was born in the little town of Bethlehem," or, "He died on a cross and supposedly rose from the dead."

The burden of evangelicals is that everyone must hear about Jesus. However, the concern is pointless. Everyone has heard about Jesus.

Muslims know about Jesus because, for them, he is a great prophet.

What do Muslims Believe About Jesus?

"Muslims believe that Jesus was not crucified. It was the plan of Jesus' enemies to crucify him, but God saved him and raised him up to Him. And the likeness of Jesus was put over another man. Jesus' enemies killed that man and crucified him, thinking that he was Jesus.

"They said, "We killed the Messiah Jesus, son of Mary, the messenger of God." They did not kill him, nor did they crucify him, but the likeness of him was put on another man (and they killed that man)." (Quran, 4:157)[11]

Muslims also believe in the virgin birth of Jesus.

Evangelicals will say, "We have to tell people about Jesus," or, "we have to declare God's love to them through Jesus." If they can get there and tell people about Jesus, they will believe and be saved. There was indeed a time when the only way people were going to hear about

---

[11] www.islam-guide.com/ch3-10.html

Jesus was if believers bodily went out and told people about him. The Apostle Paul had to go from city to city and each synagogue. Multimedia and the internet take care of that today. Almost everyone in the world has access to the internet except for those who live in the remotest regions.

Knowledge about Jesus is common in the Americas because our cultures are saturated with references to him. Everyone knows something about Christmas and Easter. As we saw in the last chapter, about 50% of the U.S. population is Christian (all groups and races). In South America, the percentage is higher at 84% (mostly Roman Catholic). I often wonder why evangelicals say, "Everyone needs to know about Jesus," as though it's something yet to accomplish. They already know about Jesus, whether they want to or not.

What they mean to say is, "We need to proselytize more people into our church, into our brand of Christianity. Today, slick marketing is used to accomplish that.

People around the world know who Jesus was. Russian and Chinese communism failed to eradicate Christianity. Many Russians returned to the Orthodox Church. Evangelicalism is growing in China. I saw a statistic some years ago that by 2020, there will be more Christians in China than in the United States. The most recent report indicates it may happen.[12]

Christians and churches are in every nation of the world, howbeit in some, a tiny percentage.

There is copious information found on the internet. A plethora of evangelical websites exist. Every denomination and most congregations have a website outlining their beliefs and programs. You could ask anyone in the world, "Who is Jesus." If, by some chance, that person didn't know about him, he or she could ask Siri, "Who is Jesus?" Siri answers, "Here's what I found: Jewish preacher and religious leader, the central figure of Christianity." More information follows and concludes, "See more on Wikipedia."

Not All Have Faith

---

[12] China Family Panel Studies (CFPS), 2012. *Published on The World Religious Cultural Issues,* 2014.

Most people know about Jesus, but not all people have faith in Jesus. Why do some people believe while others do not? It certainly is not because they haven't heard. What makes the difference? Neither intelligence nor education makes a difference. You can find people on both sides of the question who are highly intelligent and educated. The question about faith in God lies much deeper in the human experience and psyche.

People approach faith in God and the Bible, or any sacred text, in different ways. Of course, one can have faith without believing in a sacred text, but when describing Judaism, Christianity, or Islam, the two go hand in hand. They are, after all, religions of *the book*. What distinguishes fundamentalists from other believers is their unswerving faith in the sacred text. Evangelicals who have faith in Jesus must also have faith in the Bible because he is the mystical author of it. They believe in and trust it to be the inspired, inerrant, and infallible revelation from Jesus, even when they can't agree on what it teaches. All the books in it, they believe, have a cohesive message from Jesus to all people.[13] Nothing could be further from the truth. Both the Hebrew Bible and the New Testament contain books that contradict each other. The job of the evangelical or orthodox theologian is to create a cohesive message; however, it isn't there.

Back to the question: why do some people believe while others do not?

Reared in the Faith

There are those whose parents or guardians nurtured them in the Christian faith and the Bible from infancy. They grow up accepting both as part of their lives in much the same way I was accustomed to being the son of a bartender. My bedroom was on the second floor above a bar, and my window faced the street. The patrons got very noisy late on Saturday night and early Sunday morning. One hot summer night with my window open, I heard one man tell another jokingly, "I know I'm goin to hell." By the time I was in the seventh grade, it was my job to

---

[13] "In the beginning was the Word, and the Word was with God, and the Word was God. He was with God in the beginning. Through him all things were made..." (John 1-3a, TNIV). Based on the verses above and from Hebrews 1:1, the preincarnate spirit of Christ the source of revelation.

stock the beer coolers behind the bar as soon as I got off the bus from school.

I never reflected on the circumstances of my upbringing until many years later. It was part of my life. I grew up knowing what a tavern was and what it was about.

Children who grow up in a household of faith don't reflect on how their parents reared them until many years later. It is the reason children who grow up in predominantly Muslim nations accept Islam. It is part of their family and community culture. The same outcome is true for children who grow up in Roman Catholic communities. The origin of their faith isn't spiritual or intellectual. Their continuing in their parents' religion is a matter of family loyalty.

Before I became an atheist, a Catholic friend asked me why I left the Catholic faith of my parents. I had become Presbyterian.

"I no longer believed it was true," I replied.

She was as stunned by my answer as I was by her question. She said nothing after that. It was inconceivable to her that someone would leave the faith of her or his parents.

In the case of my siblings and me, we were in and out of too many churches to stick with one. Before my mother became a born-again Christian, my parents never expressed a deep commitment to any of the churches we attended. There was no denominational loyalty.

Coming of Age

Some children will arrive at adolescence and lose interest in religion, even though they go through the motions of church, synagogue, or mosque attendance. Some stop attending church and never think again about the church, God, or the Holy Text. They become apatheist persons who don't care if there's a god. That is what happened to me. When I did become a born-again Christian at age 19, it was a conscious decision and commitment.

My children attended Sunday school, worship service, and Wednesday meetings every week. My ex-wife and I laid down this rule: "as long as you're in school, you're going to attend services (college exempted)." There were appearances to maintain. The kids complied. They could see the light at the end of the tunnel. By the time the rule

33

applied to our fourth teenager, we had become sloppy about enforcement.

The Open Mind

Some attempt to approach the sacred text with an open mind. I was there too. I read some of the *Book of Mormon* before I read the Bible. I even read about the early twentieth-century psychic, Edgar Casey, thinking I might find something there. I didn't. I was searching. The open mind decides whether the story of Adam and Eve should be understood literally or figuratively. It will come across other stories that will present similar questions about the Bible's interpretation or credibility. Was the earth really created in six literal days? Is the story of Noah real? Was the whole earth flooded to the tops of the highest mountains? The open mind is untutored by religious teachers; however, someone with an open mind can also be converted. I was.

The Skeptic

Others approach the subject of God and the Bible as skeptics. They question everything that is not scientific, doubtful of testimony that assumes the supernatural—God, miracles, and a world of angels and demons. They will read the Bible critically, looking for inconsistencies, contradictions, and mythology. They dismiss stories containing miracles and events contrary to the laws of physics. God could not have created the universe and earth in six literal days. That would have to be understood figuratively at best. Can science support the testimony of a universal flood that covered the earth above the tops of the tallest mountains? All animal species couldn't have fit into the ark, even if they could have arrived there, which is impossible. The earth could not have stopped rotating for 48 hours (Joshua 10:13). Jonah could not have survived in the stomach of a fish for three days.

I was not a skeptic in the beginning; however, as I matured emotionally, I began to question, then doubt. At the end of my misguided evangelical journey, I lost the emotional need to believe. I then had to question what I believed was my whole purpose for being.

Biased to Believe

True believers are biased to believe. They might have difficulty with some of the miracles and even more difficulty with God commanding Joshua to kill every man, woman, and child of Israel's enemies, *but maybe there is a lesson behind that kind of barbarity.*

34

Perhaps the lesson is about how much God hates sin. God does not command us to do something as horrible to our fellow human beings today because *he has already punished his only Son as a substitute for sinners*; as evangelicals are inclined to say, "God hates the sin, not the sinner." Skeptics look at people in this group and wonder, "How can they be so blind?"

Blindness to reality is chosen when it can be too painful or undesirable. It is a phenomenon often seen in politics when passionate party members want something to be true when it isn't. Toward the end of the 2016 Presidential election, Donald Trump began preparing his followers for defeat by claiming the election was rigged to defeat him. No evidence was forthcoming. As I write this, his followers believe everything he says because they want to, and they have to. Otherwise, they too must question their entire worldview. Not surprisingly, many of them are evangelical fundamentalists, a group of people already operating in a fantasy world.

What skeptics may not understand about the people in this group is that they need to believe. There is something in their psyches producing the need. It may be the desire for acceptance from a group or tribe (this is where adolescents are vulnerable). Perhaps they struggle with behaviors or addictions. They find the path to recovery in God, the Bible, and church. They need to overcome what they have been convinced is *sinful behavior*. Whatever personal struggle they have, they turn to faith in God as the remedy.

The Need for Something Bigger

Others seek the meaning of life and the ultimate purpose of their lives. That was me at age nineteen. I was lost and looking for purpose and meaning, and I also developed a bias to believe. I wanted to be part of something larger than me that would change the world for good. I wanted to be part of that change. I wanted to feel I was significant.

The Zealous Proselyte

When I first attended Shelton, John, an enthusiastic, warm-hearted guy in his junior year, became my mentor. He was a Calvinist who wanted to convert the incoming class to Calvinism.[14] Moreover, he wanted us "to lead people to Christ."

He organized an evangelistic event open to students who wanted to participate. A handful of us showed up outside after dinner. He distributed gospel tracks for us to handout.

"Where are we going?" I asked.

"There's an anti-Vietnam rally at Brevard Community College.[15] That's where we're going?" He answered with his broad smile.

I was a bit confused. "Are we protesting the war?"

"We're not taking sides. We're going there to save souls." John explained we were going to hand out gospel tracts and "witness" to students if they were willing to hear.

"Walk up to anyone, hold out a tract and ask, 'Do you know Jesus Christ as your Savior?'"

We packed into a couple of cars and left. When we arrived, we located a large group of students gathered and standing in the commons area. A stage had been erected, and there were students on the platform. Someone was talking when we arrived. He introduced the president of the student council of the local high school. A kid with long hair and a beard struggling to sprout stood behind a mic bobbing his head up and down in a "hey-dude" attitude, grinned, and made the peace sign with his right hand.

"Peace."

Students cheered.

He continued talking. The crowd applauded and hooted approval. We ignored him, spread through the standing assembly, and handed out tracts. Some kids took them. Others refused. Others, quite understandably, expressed disapproval about us being there. I felt like we were crashing a party which we were. An antagonist started asking me combative questions. I answered them as best I could. Another

---

[14] Calvinism is another name for the teaching that God chose people for salvation before the beginning of time. The sixteenth century French theologian, John Calvin, as a chief proponent of this teaching.

[15] Currently Eastern Florida State University

student joined with more objections and questions. Three and then four students joined what became a debate. I turned to see a crowd of about a dozen gathering around me. Instead of feeling surrounded and overwhelmed, I was sky-high with emotion and excitement.

A kid asked, "I'm Jewish. Are you sayn' I'm goin to hell if I don't believe in Jesus?"

"That's right," I said with conviction.

That brought groans, protests, and nasty words.

Someone stumped me with a question I couldn't answer. The little crowd started breaking up. I didn't know the Jewish guy had gotten on stage. Someone handed him the mic.

"Hey," his words came over the mic. "A guy over there," pointing in my direction, "told me I'm going to hell because I'm Jewish."

"No! Boo. Get 'em outa here. Go away," kids in the crowd started shouting.

Someone from our group grabbed me by the elbow and said, "Come on. We're going."

The whole time this had occurred, I felt elated and "full of the Holy Spirit." I had never been so excited or felt so spiritually transported to another place. I told our group what had happened. They already knew. I was on cloud nine on the way back to our little campus. As Steve Martin's character said in the movie *The Jerk*, I found my special purpose.

John's eyes glittered with cheerfulness as he smiled. We did it! Though we made no converts, we *witnessed*.

Faith in God enabled me to transcend my mundane, flawed, and meaningless life. Or so I thought.

Chapter 4

Immortality: Transcending Death

Death is always bad news, no doubt about it, but it is a reality we must face. Everything that lives dies, and everything that lives will fight to stay alive. Have you ever caught a fish in a stream or lake? It will struggle to pull away or dislodge the hook. Instinct takes over, and the fish expends every ounce of energy to escape death. Have you ever caught a mouse in a trap that didn't die? Though nearly dead, as soon as it sees or hears you coming, it will make one last and futile attempt to escape. It is true of every living thing.

As a pastor, I sat beside people approaching death. They believed in Jesus and the resurrection; nevertheless, they struggled to avoid meeting him in person. They resisted to the last long breath, even after they were unconscious and unable to eat and drink for days. To struggle to stay alive to the point of complete exhaustion is instinctual in every living thing. Given normal circumstances and positive mental health, we don't want to die. We dread death.

Humans may not be the only animals who contemplate mortality. Perhaps other mammals with higher functioning brains—porpoises, whales, elephants, and other primates—also contemplate death. They grieve the loss of their companions. However, humans have something more. We have highly developed and vivid imaginations to make illusions real. As we contemplate our mortality, we also imagine life in some form after death. Then we agree that what we have concocted is true. We can't prove immortality, but we can believe in and approve of it. Our collective mind has created life after death and sealed it in sacred texts.

Those who have lost loved ones experience a *need* to believe in the afterlife. They carry with them the hope they will see their loved ones again. The preacher often says, "They [the dead] are in a better place," or "they're looking down on us today." For the record, I never said those things. My unspoken policy was never to place the deceased in heaven or hell. I left that to family, friends, or those less fond of the departed. In my experience as a pastor, people imagine heaven as a family reunion.

Meeting Jesus has little to do with it except his being the one who gets them there.

Often, I was asked to officiate the funeral of someone I never met. The survivors had no church of their own, but they had a friend who attended ours.

"Would your pastor do the funeral service?"

Sometimes my services were offered before someone made a request.

"I'll ask our pastor. He'll do that for your family. I'm sure."

I always did. How could I say no? It was an opportunity to promote the church. Maybe the family of the deceased or someone attending the service would come to church on Sunday. Of course, I was paid for officiating the funeral—not much, but some. Seriously, I did derive a sense of satisfaction by providing solace to a grieving family. I had officiated and attended services of tragic loss and inconsolable grief, especially when the deceased was young, or a parent left behind young children. Survivors understandably want to believe they will see their departed loved ones again. The hope is that one of the primal urges that contribute to faith in God.

When I officiated, I made time for family or friends to say something about the departed. The practice is customary, and there are always those who have something to say. It helps survivors and friends come to terms with the loss of their loved ones. It works for people who believe in life after death and for those who don't. It is the final ritual of collective memory, an effort to smile amid grief, comfort each other, and say good-bye.

There are eulogies—praise for the deceased. Some are moving, while others can be amusing when they depict the departed as active in heaven. When the deceased is elderly, and death is natural, there is always some humor. There should be. It is part of the grieving process.

"Mom is baking pies for God."

"Hank is building mansions for us in heaven."

"Aunt Harriet is feeding the birds in God's aviary."

They are always doing things—cutting grass, trimming trees, continuing to pursue their occupations or hobbies. God has lots of stuff that needs tending.

All the departed go to heaven, even the stinkers. No one goes to hell. You are never going to hear a preacher say, "Unfortunately, Jake must be in hell."

Belief in an afterlife does not necessitate belief in God, but it usually does. The afterlife exists in a mystery the believer cannot comprehend. Some believe the souls of the departed are with us. They appear as birds, rainbows, or specters we see from the corner of one eye. They are there. They are here. They are looking down on us. Belief in the afterlife is one of the more harmless aspects of faith and religion.

If there is a God who makes the dead alive again, it doesn't have to be the god described in the Bible, the Quran, or any other religious text. Belief in the afterlife is born of imagination. I would never intentionally disrespect anyone who believes in it. Belief in the afterlife reveals our desire to escape death and achieve immortality. Early in our hominid evolution, it contributed to religion—the transcendence of death.

Perhaps another way of looking at our need to believe in the afterlife is the need for personal continuity. We awake in the morning, go about our day, eat our meals, and go to sleep at night, anticipating the next day. We want people to remember us; we can continue in that way. Do you want people to remember you? Be a good person. Love the people you know, treat them well, and make them laugh.

My half-Irish grandmother was a superstitious soul who believed in ghosts and claimed to have seen one. As a young woman, she woke one night with a startle and saw a ghost with a red beard sitting on the edge of her bed.

"After I'm gone," she told us, kids, more than once, "you'll think about me, and when you do, I'll be there."

Geez! Creeps me out every time.

"Hi, Grandma."

Chapter 5

Fear

"With primitive man, it is above all fear that evokes religious notions—fear of hunger, wild beasts, sickness, death. Since at this stage of existence, understanding of causal connections is usually poorly developed, the human mind creates for itself more or less analogous beings on whose wills and actions these fearful happenings depend." [16]

--Albert Einstein

Some children and prospects are frightened into faith when they're told to fear the punishment of hellfire if they don't accept Jesus as their savior. Yes, that is still taught and preached. I listened to a well know English preacher on a CD. He said unless one is converted by the fear of hellfire, that conversion is not genuine. The CD was given to me by someone who had been attending church for a while. I returned it to her without comment.

A lady in my last congregation lamented her grown son was no longer a Christian. He no longer cared. "I don't understand," she said. "As a child, he accepted Jesus as his savior at youth camp during an evangelistic meeting. I was there. I saw it."

"Did the preacher tell the children they would go to hell if they didn't believe and come forward to accept Jesus?" I asked.

"Yes."

"Then, of course, he believed. Fear isn't a good motivator. It's like using the threat of torture to get someone to do something they don't want to do." It leads only to the person's resentment.

When I was beginning to believe, I first read the *Gospel According to Luke*. The book contains many parables and pithy retorts spoken by Jesus. I liked the style, and the name Luke was close to mine—

---

[16] New York Times Magazine, Nov. 9, 1930 pp.1-4

not a good reason. Jesus talked about hell a lot, more than any other character in the Bible.

Soon, I found myself reading the *Book of Revelation*, also called *The Apocalypse of John*. The book intrigued me.

Hal Lindsey published *The Late Great Planet Earth*, a book that was very popular at the time and a bestseller in 1970. Lindsey highlighted the frightening predictions found in *Revelations* for those who did not repent and believe. The world was going to end very soon, and not with a whimper but a bang, so hurry up. The end will be cataclysmic and terrifying. You don't want to be left behind when the *rapture* occurs. That's when believers will be caught up into heaven before the beginning of the seven-year tribulation.

Perhaps you've seen the bumper sticker: "In case of rapture, this vehicle will be driverless." Ha! Ha!

Jesus doesn't return in peace and with gentleness, but in vengeance and with a sword. The angel swings its sickle and reaps the grapes (people), and casts them into the great winepress of God's wrath (Rev. 14:19). Why would the angel use a sickle to reap grapes? Don't question, only believe.

Seven bowls of God's wrath are poured out on the inhabitants of the earth—festering sores, the sea turns to blood, the sun scorches people with fire, and "people gnaw their tongues in agony and curse God" (Rev. 16:10, NIV). Jesus returns with an army of angels. He wears a robe dipped in blood. A sharp sword comes out of his mouth to strike down the nations (Rev. 20:14, 15).

There is a lot of symbolism in the book, and one of the themes is Jesus taking vengeance on those who persecuted the "saints," believers. There is no end to the bloodshed and the torment of those who accept the *mark of the beast* (666). And so it goes.

I lay on my bed reading and became afraid of God. I saw myself being judged. What if Jesus came tonight? What would happen to me? Was I believing these things because the Bible and the Christian faith are so ancient? There was no one to show me why I should question what I read, who wrote the book and why, or what were the Jewish apocalyptic sources behind it. There was nothing I could find to critique it. Of course, many criticisms of Biblical literature were available, but they were in university libraries. There was no internet.

Fear did its work, but not the fear of hell by itself, but the fear of God who created hell. "I say unto you, my friends," Jesus said to the crowd, "don't be afraid of those who kill the body, and after that have no more that they can do. But I will forewarn you whom you will fear: fear him, who after he has killed, has the power to cast into Gehenna. Yes, I say to you, fear him" (Lk 12:4-5). He is none other than God.

By the time I was nearing the end of my ministry, I was contemplating the many theological and logical problems associated with God's judgment and hellfire. I knew that fear was not an appropriate or effective method for leading people to Jesus, especially not in the twenty-first century. I was questioning some Scriptures without realizing the consequences. I had passed beyond the gates of mindless fear and began to trust my thoughts and develop independent convictions. If something doesn't seem right, it probably isn't. If something doesn't make sense, it probably doesn't.

After the sermon one Sunday, while people were chatting with each other ("fellowshipping"), a lady approached me and wanted to tell me something. "Do you know what we need more of in preaching?" I didn't try to answer her question because I didn't know, and I knew she was going to tell me. I just looked at her and raised my eyebrows, waiting for her to answer her question.

"Hell. We need preaching about hell," She said sweetly and sincerely. The disposition of sweetness and the topic of hell seem incongruous. There was no lecture or rebuke. She was offering encouragement to preach about hell with no explanation.

I gave no response. I was over it. I might have made a sound like, "Umm," with a nod, and moved on. I didn't know how else to respond. I sure as hell wasn't going to preach about hell.

Believers are terrified to doubt. They are afraid of *apostasy— falling away.* Doubt will lead to unbelief, and that will lead to hell. There are plenty of dreadful warnings in the New Testament.

For if after they have escaped the pollutions of the world through the knowledge of the Lord and Savior Jesus Christ, they are again entangled therein, and overcome, the latter end is worse with them than the beginning. For it had been better for them not to have known the way of righteousness, than, after they have known it, to turn from the holy commandment delivered unto them. 2 Peter 2:20-21 (NIV)

43

Within the context, "they" are false prophets (2:1). But as we can see from the passage, they didn't begin that way. Initially, they escaped the pollutions of the world by faith in Christ. Peter warned of true prophets turned false. The author of *Hebrews* threatens another kind of believer who is in danger: the one who keeps on sinning.

If we deliberately keep on sinning after we have received the knowledge of the truth, no sacrifice for sins is left, but only a fearful expectation of judgment and of raging fire that will consume the enemies of God. Hebrews 10:26-27 (NIV)

What will happen to you if you're a believer and you keep on sinning? This passage seems clear enough: if you don't stop sinning, you're going to hell. However, what is sinning? The gerund, *sinning,* is from the Greek noun *hamartos,* which means *missing the mark, falling short*. In the New Testament, *missing the target* is always determined by the context. In Hebrews Chapter 10, the unknown author exhorts believers to "draw near to God with a sincere heart in full assurance of faith" (verse 21); to "hold unswervingly to the hope we profess" (verse 23), "not giving up meeting together" (verse 25).

The *sin* seems to be falling away from the faith and any of the ways that may be understood, from renouncing the faith to simply becoming a lazy Christian who doesn't care anymore and skips worship services. Fear of falling away creates anxiety for the believer who cares; consequently, anxiety never ends.

Chapter 6

How Can All Those People Be Wrong?

Large, ancient, and highly organized Christian groups of people welcome and guide new converts. These groups are called churches. They have been with us for almost 2,000 years.

Between the third to sixth centuries, the orthodox Christian church succeeded in suppressing all other competing Christian groups in the Mediterranean world. Within the same period, it also constructed its Bible, the New Testament. It shaped a theology by the end of the fourth century, to which the sixteenth-century Protestant Reformers largely adhered 1,200 years later.

The orthodox church split in the ninth century into what is now the Roman Catholic Church and the Eastern Orthodox Churches.[17] The Catholic Church united the kingdoms of Europe under one church and its leader, the Pope of Rome. The language of the church was Latin, which also became the diplomatic, legal, and educational language of Europe. The Bible was translated into Latin by Jerome in the fourth century and became known as the *Vulgate* (meaning *for the people*), the only translation in use until the Reformation. The church established the first great universities in Europe. It founded hospitals and orphanages. Monks in monastery scriptoriums throughout Europe copied Greek and Latin manuscripts of the Bible, literature, and philosophy.

Across two millennia, volumes of theologies, church histories, commentaries, and devotional works written by brilliant men and women have filled libraries. The accounts of great evangelists, missionaries, and reformers are innumerable. Who could help but not be impressed by so great a witness of so many Godly, noble, and intelligent people? I was. The church's antiquity and authority create an illusion of rock-solid credibility. People want to believe in ancient, established, and respected

---

[17] The Orthodox Church has several branches: Greek, Russians, Romanian, Ethiopian, etc. Other churches, like the Chaldean in Iraq, the Coptic in Egypt and the Eritrean in Ethiopia, developed independently.

institutions trusted by millions of people for hundreds of years. The Church established itself in the hearts and minds of people of all socio-economic backgrounds and levels of education.

I believe the Christian Church served its purpose up to the Age of Reason in the eighteenth century. Secularism would begin to take over most institutions and do a much better job guiding humanity. The church also had its very dark side when it controlled the societies and governments of Europe. Those who opposed or even departed from its teachings were persecuted, tortured, or gruesomely executed. Children were not exempt from the bloody persecutions that broke out. (Search for more about the Massacre of the Waldensian at Merindol in 1545, in southern France).

The church was a constant presence in people's lives from the cradle to the grave, from baptism to last rites. For the few who could afford it, the church provided all education from childhood to the university. It taught everyone, even the illiterate, how to understand the world and what to believe. Preaching in the churches was, and still is, a form of education. The church was the ultimate authority on everything.

It taught the creation of the cosmos by God in six literal days. He made human beings in his image. He rested on the seventh day. Any merging of natural science with faith was understood in light of the church's teachings based on the Word of God and church tradition. Its interpretation of the Bible became the foundation of theology and medieval philosophy. Any scholar, astronomer, author, or scientist who disagreed with the Church faced condemnation, the loss of employment, prison, torture, and even death. The Church destroyed the works of scientists who disagreed with its interpretation of reality.

The great works of Renaissance art highlighted Biblical themes. Among the greatest of these were the paintings of Michelangelo, Leonardo Da Vinci, and Raphael. The constant topics were the lives of biblical characters, especially the Madonna. The artists' purpose was to illustrate humankind's dependence on God and to give him all the glory. The works of literature—epic poems, musical lyrics, street theatre, and histories—were all religious. Two of the greatest epic poems, Dante's *Inferno* and John Milton's *Paradise Lost*, explored people's relationship with God and the ultimate human destinies of heaven or hell.

Ironically, higher education, the use of reason, and critical thinking ultimately undermined the Church's credibility and authority. The Renaissance sowed the seeds of skepticism through the study of physical sciences and the critique of sacred texts. The intellectuals trained by the church in its universities challenged its time-honored traditions. The Renaissance led to the Reformation, and the Catholic Church began to lose its social and political dominance in Europe.

However, even after the Reformation, the Bible was believed to be the inerrant Word of God, extending its authority over every aspect of life. Not until the eighteenth century did the Christian worldview begin to lose its grip over the minds of educated Europeans and Americans. The most apparent result of the loss of religious influence was the ratification of the Constitution of the United States in 1788, producing a government non-committal to religion, allowing religious freedom for all. Political discourse became rational and secular, and by the twentieth century, it began to dominate popular thinking.

Could all those people, all those brilliant religious thinkers, and artists be wrong for so many centuries? That is the same rhetorical question someone could have posed to Martin Luther about the Catholic Church in 1517. It is the same question that could have been asked of American revolutionaries in 1776, the same question the leaders of the slave states would have argued in 1860.

Yes, our ancestors were often wrong about many things; that is why we don't have a state religion, slavery, or believe the sun revolves around the earth.

From Absolute Authority to Slick Marketing

The church remains a vast community in the United States and many other countries, comprising thousands of local church communities and millions of believers. People are no longer coerced to be Christian. With freedom and the absence of persecution, churches today compete for members. Especially among non-Catholics, denominational loyalties have disappeared. The churches learned how to make corrections to their teachings and practices. When church memberships dwindled, leaders were compelled to learn how to market the church and its message effectively.

The trend was not to resuscitate the traditional church with its older members who clung to their nineteenth-century hymnals and pipe organs. Young evangelistic pastors with vision targeted the younger un-churched individuals and families, offering contemporary music and programs for every age group.

At the time I began my ministry in a small traditional church in a village in Michigan, a young man two years my junior, Rick Warren, founded Saddleback Church in Lake Forest, Californian, in 1980. There was nothing traditional about Saddleback. Rick held praise services in a gymnasium. Instead of an organ belting out old-time hymns, drums, guitars, and praise-team vocalists led the congregation in music. Rick wore jeans and a casual shirt. Participants came dressed as they were— no suits, jackets, or ties on men or dresses on women. The church grew exponentially and became a model for start-up churches across North America.

Rick's message has always been positive and practical, focusing on how to help believers live meaningful and productive lives. The churches following his lead grew into megachurches with Sunday attendance in the tens of thousands. He changed the face of the church while maintaining the core teachings of evangelicalism. Saddleback belongs to the Southern Baptist Convention. Today about 22,000 people attend Sunday services at Saddleback, and it now has multiple campuses.

Megachurches don't grow by proselytizing but by attracting Christians to leave their smaller local churches. The older meeting places are too small, and the congregations too poor to offer the amenities of larger churches with large campuses.

The draw of megachurches is analogous to *the Wall Marts* of America sucking the life out of the mom and pop stores now dead on Main Street or the country corner. Megachurches resemble large corporations and employ large, full-time staff with benefits. Professional controllers manage the church's finances. Professional musicians lead worship services. A team of multiple pastors attends various aspects of the church's ministry.

People drive 30 to 50 miles to churches that offer everything— junior church, youth activity rooms with pool tables, gymnasiums, and café's offering **Café Au Lait**. As a pastor, I talked to adults looking for a new church. They told me their children would decide where to attend.

However, in their efforts to make themselves attractive, churches have unhinged themselves from traditional, biblical beliefs and practices they once emphasized. In each generation, the Bible is used and interpreted differently. If you attended a revival meeting in the 1970s, the preacher would have told you the gaping jaws of hell awaited if you didn't walk down the aisle and accept Jesus as your Lord and savior. You'll see messages like that printed on highway billboards, especially when driving through the south.

Today, evangelical pastors preach Christ and the gospel as the way of finding true happiness and living a fuller life. Healing addictions and sinful behaviors are additional benefits. Some changes are positive as churches provide more resources to help people in areas of their lives that matter—giving material assistance when communities are devastated by natural disasters or by providing emotional support to communities terrorized by unnatural mass-shootings.

Evangelicals have become less offensive and slicker in their delivery. You will hear about the love and acceptance of God—"God hates sin, not the sinner." You won't hear about hell. You will hear about the wonderful peace and joy that comes through "having a relationship with Jesus." He is the healer of your anxiety, depression, addiction, self-loathing, guilt, and loneliness. Whatever afflicts you, Jesus will put you on the road to healing and a more meaningful life. Even better, you will receive the gift of eternal life—a false message still, but the new one is better than the old. At least it's positive.

The emphasis is on keeping the gospel simple and attractive. Don't condemn anyone for anything. God forgives, and so should you. God loves people of all ages, races, genders, and sexual preferences. God loves the LGBTQ community, and so should believers. "Because," evangelicals believe, "if we can lead them to a relationship with Jesus Christ, he will heal them of their sexual perversity." The threat of hell still exists, but no one talks about it openly.

Of course, evangelicals still insist the Bible is the Word of God, but they avoid the repelling messages and stories offensive to twenty-first-century sensibilities. This shift in approach has a counter effect on the church, progressively disconnecting it from the Bible. Evangelicalism has become less dogmatic.

CityFest 2018

On September 8 and 9, 2018, the *Luis Palau Association* brought an evangelistic presentation to Grand Rapids, Michigan, with the support and cooperation of 435 churches. The event, titled *CityFest,* attracted 18,000 adults and children with 78,000 "watching worldwide," according to its website; however, the website reported the attendance as 30,000, of which 1,830 people "decided to follow Jesus Christ."[18]

Luis was born in Argentina and became part of the Billy Graham crusade decades ago. At age 83, he announced he had stage four lung cancer while he expressed the joy of his faith and his hope for healing. His son, Andrew, the heir-apparent of the Palau organization, spoke at the closing event of the assembly and delivered a classic Billy Graham style sermon and "altar call."

Throughout Saturday and Sunday, Christian rock bands and singers entertained young crowds, parents, and chaperones. Justin Beiber was there, unannounced in the backstage area. He is reported to be friends with the speaker's family. He served as window dressing; there, just chillin with em. Word quickly circulated via Twitter. Some teens were able to get autographs.

Here are some excerpts from Luis's introduction and Andrew's message.

Luis:

"It's been a great life, thanks to Jesus Christ, the Son of God. Jesus Christ is a mighty God, and he wants to come into your life and change your life, and it's a beautiful life. There is an enemy, and he's called Satan. Look around and look at the broken homes. Look at the young people who take their lives. Why? Because they don't have Christ living in them."

---

[18]Palau.org/events-grand rapids, September 8-9, 2018. The meetings were set up in many cities through the states. You can find the scheduled past events and future events on their website.

He introduced Andrew.

Andrew:

"That peace and prosperity we're seeking after it [for Grand Rapids], we're praying for it, but we also know that the peace and prosperity that my dad was talking about, that we've been singing about, it only comes into the life of a man or a woman when we enter into a relationship with the living God through Jesus Christ. I'm going to invite you tonight. Your life will never be the same, and this is what Jesus Christ promises, he says, I will revolutionize your life. Isn't that amazing? There's someone else here, and he's lurking around, and his name is Satan and the enemy of your soul. That's what Satan is, the enemy of your soul, and he stands in his kingdom of darkness, and he lies to you. He's a liar, and he is the father of all lies."

Andrew went on to tell how he trashed his life every night on drugs and alcohol when he attended the University of Oregon in Eugene. I stopped there. I assume he was going to talk about that until Jesus saved him. I forwarded the YouTube video to the altar-call, where he first quoted the cosmic Jesus of Revelation 3:20: "Look, I stand at the door, and knock. If any man hears my voice and opens the door, I will come in to him and will dine with him, and he with me" (KJV) The context doesn't matter—it is now. The invitation of Jesus is vital and relevant. Here is the alter-call to receive Jesus as Savior. All eyes are shut.

Andrew:

"Just say to him, Heavenly Father. I love you. I believe in you. Thank you for never giving up on me. Please forgive me. I am so sorry. Clean me out. Take all the garbage and the darkness. Lord, clean me out. Give me a fresh start. Forgive me. Thank you for paying that heavy price. Thank you for forgiving me. I believe in you, and I receive you now. Come into my life. Fill me with your Holy Spirit because I need power I have not had before. Thank you for coming in, and thank you for heaven, my home—what a gift. Father, I am your child. I come to you, and I will never fear death again because I know when I die, I will be with you there forever. Thank you and show me now; show me what to do. I want to walk with you and live the abundant life. Heal me. Transform me. Lift the darkness off my life, Lord. I want to walk in the life and experience the beauty and the joy

51

of life with you, from now to the finish. I'm yours forever. In Jesus' name. Amen."

Eyes opened, and Andrew extended his hand, palm up. "How many of you invited Jesus into your life," he asked. "I need to know so I can pray for you." There are other reasons, too. There were hoots and hollers here and there from teens as some raised their hands. "Keep your hands up, and counselors in orange jackets will get you some postcard questionnaires, and we have these booklets to give you of John's Gospel."

The crowd of kids and chaperones, however, pressed the counselors against the stage, and because there were no aisles, the counselors couldn't move, so questionnaires and gospels were passed into the crowd. Enthusiasm waned as the video closed. I don't think it ended as smoothly as intended.

The message went beyond the Bible; Andrew threw in a few biblical phrases to keep the message a little tethered to the Bible. "Clean me out," however, is not one of them. The appeal was emotional: your life is a mess, but Jesus will clean out the mess and give you an abundant, joyful life. Beware, Satan lurks, even here in front of the Gerald Ford museum and on the banks of Grand River. He stands in his kingdom. *Fear of Satan* is a tool to drive one into the protective arms of Jesus. There was no mention of the terrors of hell. It's all about finding an abundant, prosperous life.

Could all those people be wrong? Yes. They are wrong. It's the twenty-first century; Satan isn't lurking anywhere or standing in his kingdom.

I remember the chief sales lesson when I became an insurance salesman—*emotion sells,* so does the fear of risk. Fear is the tool of the rhetorician in religion and politics.

Chapter 7

Teaching the Mysteries

The church, in its various forms, has existed for centuries to welcome new converts into its fellowship. However, more than coffee and donuts are needed. The initiate will be introduced (indoctrinated) in the practices and teachings of the church, i.e., its *interpretation* of the Bible.

Theology means the *study of God,* but it goes beyond exploring the nature of God. In college and seminary, I learned the *loci* (points) of theology, which answered questions. What is revelation? What is the Bible, and how does it reveal God to us? What is a human being? Who is Jesus Christ? How are humans saved from sin and death? The questions and topics extend to many areas. I'm not going to list them here. Theology is a logically organized compilation of *truths* drawn from the Bible to make the Bible appear to have a consistent message from God. The historical contexts and themes of the biblical documents are all over the place; theology attempts to bring them together as a cohesive message.

Evangelicals imagine all 66 documents in both testaments agree on God's message. To understand the message, a knowledgeable Christian must show you because you cannot understand the Bible on your own.

A few months after my born-again conversion, I read the first four chapters of Romans over and over, trying to grasp the argument. It wasn't like anything I read before. I was going solo. If I had given it more time, I might have pondered why Luke and John's gospels were so different and why Jesus was portrayed so differently in each book.

The first day I arrived at Shelton College, I joined the other students in the cafeteria for dinner. Enough kids were friendly and made me feel welcomed. Because it was such a small school, everyone was going to know each other. That's when I first met John.

"Hey, you gotta come to the hymn-sing tonight," he said with exuberance.

As the cafeteria cleared out, I went to my room and thought about it. The music I liked came from the Beatles and the Rolling Stones, not Isaac Watts. I hadn't attended a church since my family left the Episcopal Church in Crown Point. They didn't have hymn-sings, nor did the Catholics. I never sang hymns with a group of kids before. I decided to go. I was curious and lonely.

As I approached the auditorium, I paused. I could hear the kids singing old-time, fast-tempo gospel songs like *What Can Wash Away My Sins*. I got an odd sensation and felt like I was maybe in the wrong place. A little voice in my head said, "Run. Get out of here." But I didn't. Maybe that was Satan talking.

I stepped forward and opened the door, and music flooded out. The students were singing in the lobby of the auditorium. Vocal harmonics lured me in; kids looked at me with welcoming smiles. I sat down and, within minutes, joined right in. I would be singing hymns every day in chapel for the next four years and participating in group prayer every night in the dorm. It all became part of active mental reorientation—the acceptance of and submission to brainwashing.

Some kids attended Shelton because their parents coerced them. Enough of them were there because they wanted to be, and now I was one of them. I made many friends. When I returned home for Christmas vacation, I was a different person. I had become a zealot. I wanted to make sure every person in my family heard the gospel, as my new friends had taught me to do.

That's how it works. You take one step, then another, and before you know it, you're in the belly of the beast, lured in by acceptance, love, and friendship. It's probably like that with every cult.

Esoteric

An evangelical friend said to me, "The Bible is pretty clear." But is it? One cannot say anything about the Bible as a single document because it's a collection of different books written by many authors across one thousand years. "But," evangelicals say, "God is the author." They mean to say the Bible has a single cohesive message; however, it doesn't.

What do the authors of the biblical books say? What did Jesus say? It depends on which Jesus you read.

Jesus told his disciples the parable of the seed and the sower. The meaning of the parable was not clear until he explained it to his disciples. He said to them, "To you it has been given to know the mystery of the kingdom of God; but to those who are outside, all things come in parables, so that "Seeing they may see and not perceive and hearing they may hear and not understand." (Mark 4:11,12; Mt. 13:11, KJV). Jesus quoted from Isaiah 6:9.

The Gospel According to John has Jesus saying something very different to the crowd in Jerusalem.

Jesus was walking in the temple, in the colonnade of Solomon. So the Jews gathered around him and said to him, "How long will you keep us in suspense? If you are the Christ, tell us plainly." Jesus answered them, "I told you, and you do not believe. (Jn. 10:23-25, ESV).

In *John's Gospel*, Jesus spoke plainly; he was clear about what he said. He never hid his conviction that he is the divine Messiah. We will look at the rest of this dialogue from another angle in Chapter 8. In John's account, Jesus never speaks in parables.

Many writings in the Bible describe its meaning as esoteric, i.e., deep and mysterious, spiritual knowledge intended for and understood by the cult. A person cannot fully understand it until trained teachers and mentors clarify it. It is "the faith which was once and for all time delivered to the saints" (Jude 3). The passage refers to oral tradition, the teaching handed down to each generation. Reading the Bible and understanding its *true meaning* requires a special kind of instruction. One must be shown the *correct interpretation*; after all, the correct interpretation could make the difference between being a Catholic, a Presbyterian, or a Jehovah's Witness.

You can see the esoteric nature of Christian teaching in the biblical narrative of Phillip encountering the Ethiopian official on the road in his chariot. He was reading about the *suffering servant* in Isaiah 53:7-8.

"Do you understand what you are reading?" Phillip asked. "How can I unless someone guides me," the official replied. "Then Phillip opening his mouth and beginning with this Scripture told him the good news of Jesus" (Acts 8:30,31,35 RSV).

Again, in Acts 18:24-28—Aquila and Priscilla were a Jewish Christian couple from Rome who met Paul in the city of Corinth, Greece. During their time with Paul, he improved their understanding of the faith, as taught by him. Paul left them in Ephesus, Asia Minor, where they had moved on. He then departed for Jerusalem.

Aquila and Priscilla encountered Apollos, a Christian evangelist and a native of Alexandria. He knew nothing about Paul. The couple heard him and noticed he "spoke and taught *accurately* the things concerning Jesus, though he knew only the *baptism of John*" (18:25, RSV).

Apollos went on to speak in the synagogue on the Sabbath. Priscilla and Aquila heard him preach, but they noticed his teaching needed some correction. "They took him [aside] and expounded to him the way of God *more accurately.*" It appears his message was not as accurate as Paul's. There was no single coherent teaching about the *Way*. We don't know what is meant by "he only knew the baptism of John."

In all fairness, there was, as yet, no New Testament, so it was Paul's version of the *Way of God*. There may have been some writings, but we don't know of any. In fact, at that point, Paul had not convinced the rest of the church of his teaching about Jesus Christ. There was no uniform gospel message in the church. Christians were interpreting the Scriptures (the Hebrew Bible) from the traditions they received (word of mouth); naturally, there were many different messages.

Even with the New Testament completed and a plethora of information available online, the practice of teaching the novice the correct interpretation continues to this day, as strong as ever. I did that in the adult Sunday school class for most of my 28 years as a pastor. One really cannot be left to form his or her private interpretation; when one is, a new denomination may be born. That is what has happened historically.

Information alone cannot replace the mentor-protégé relationship.

Chapter 8

Experiencing the Spirit

Evangelicals believe religious instruction from a trained teacher is not enough for the novice to understand the gospel message; a profound spiritual experience from the Holy Spirit is necessary. The Spirit is the primary teacher.

One must experience being born again by the Holy Spirit to have him as a teacher. The new birth is an emotional breakthrough, an epiphany, and enlightenment, leading to a saving knowledge about Christ. For an evangelical, the imagined experience becomes the assurance of salvation and proof of God's existence and presence.

If you try to show an evangelical the contradictions in the Bible, he won't look at them, or he'll look past them. He will stubbornly maintain his faith in the Bible as the Word of God. "I'll have to research that," he may say, or, "I'll have to ask my pastor." he never bothers because of one thing he is sure— "Jesus is real because he is in my life."

John and Maddie were going through a marital crisis. John was spending all his time helping his father with the farm after his full-time day job. Even though his father also had a full-time job, he had to keep the farm going. (It's a farmer thing that only they understand. They say it's in their blood).

Maddie had come from a Baptist church-going family. She believed if John started attending church, he would be born again, and that would save his soul and their marriage.

They came to the worship service on Sunday. That's how we met. After the service, she told me they needed counseling. I was always willing to do what I could. She shared with me that if things didn't change, she couldn't stay in the marriage much longer. Also, there were tensions between her and the in-laws. She was also putting pressure on John to become a born-again Christian.

I met with them. The problems on the surface were as Maggie had described. John was experiencing a great deal of stress. He would not abandon helping his father with the farm, but something had to change. Maybe he could change.

In the minds of many evangelicals, becoming born again will begin to fix everything.

One evening I got a call.

"Pastor, I have to talk to you tonight. Can you come to the apartment?" He sounded excited like he had discovered something.

I never said "no" to anyone in the church. When I arrived, he met me in the parking lot and asked to talk to me in the car. I didn't understand why, but I nodded in agreement.

"What is it, John?" I asked.

"When I pulled up to the apartment and turned off the car, I saw this flash of light," he began, paused, and continued, "and heard the voice of God."

After ten seconds of silence and trying not to sound doubtful, I asked, "What did he say?" I was skeptical. I had never heard the voice of God. My concern was he might have experienced a neurological disorder.

"He said my name, 'John.' That was all. I know it was him, just know it."

I let him talk about his experience. I had to be encouraging. At my urging, we went up to the apartment to join Maggie; I wanted to include her in this. We sat around the table and talked about what happened to John. She knew. She had encouraged him to call me.

The only thing I could think to do was instruct him in the next steps. His spiritual life was only beginning. Maybe. Of course, I prayed with them and thanked the Lord for his conversion.

John had experienced a cathartic breakthrough, not unlike the one I had many years before. I needed to be credulous and encouraging. He believed God had changed him. He was born again. Unfortunately, John and Maggie set aside the more deep-seated issues between them.

They attended services regularly and were excited about his new faith. Within a few months, however, the thrill waned, as it usually does, and he returned to being himself. More substantive issues persisted, and family tensions remained. Maggie finally realized she could not change him, his family, or what she didn't like in their marriage.

They stopped attending worship services and avoided my calls.

I learned later he had begun seeing a single woman in the church he had dated years before. He and Maggie separated, and the marriage ended in divorce.

Over the years, I met men who started attending church services because they thought it would somehow save their marriage when it was already too late.

Another young man, Freddy, finished roofing the house I bought after I left the ministry. He was a hard worker but struggled with substance abuse. One day he came to work with a big smile.

"Pastor," he said excitedly, "I'm born-again!"

Freddy had had a full-blown experience with Jesus. The Holy Spirit became his new addiction.

By that time, I hadn't been a pastor for several years and was no longer a believer, but I played along. "Great," I said with a slight smile. Freddy had a crisis and found his break-through. He experienced Jesus. He was attending a charismatic church where members spoke in tongues and saw things; they had waking visions.

The following Monday, he came to work still high on God. He told me how, in the worship service, he was seated with his mentor-friend and saw vapor rising some rows ahead. He whispered to his friend, "Did you see that?

"No," his friend replied. "What did you see?"

"I saw vapor rising just above the heads of those people," pointing to them, "then it disappeared. What was it?

"The Holy Spirit," his friend assured him without hesitation.

If you attend a church where believers see visions and speak in tongues, you will eventually do both if you want to.

Charismatic pastors and communities who believe in speaking in tongues, visions of God, and healing encourage those kinds of experiences. They are not emphasized as much in some churches as it is in others. While many evangelical churches are not charismatic, they continue to emphasize the importance of spiritual experiences as evidence of having a relationship with Jesus.

The Old Testament

In the Psalm, King David describes God's protection and deliverance from his enemies. God sustains him; he is with him in spirit. He encourages David when he is pursued by the wicked who seek his demise. He is comforted in the loss of his son, born to Bathsheba.

His most dramatic and life-changing experience is his repentance for committing adultery with Bathsheba and sending her husband into an ambush that took his life. Psalm 6 and 51 express not only the heartfelt remorse of his sin but also the joy of experiencing God's forgiveness, restoration, and transformation.

Let me hear joy and gladness; that the bones you have broken rejoice. Create in me a clean heart, O God, and renew a right spirit within me. Cast me not away from your presence, and take not your holy spirit from me. Restore to me the joy of your salvation and uphold me with a willing spirit. (Psalm 51:8,10-11, ESV)

David entered the crisis of his life—the guilt of adultery and murder, mental torture aggravated by the incriminating words of Nathan the prophet. David was in the crucible of his life and discovered the catharsis of repentance, followed by the exhilaration of forgiveness and the joy of restoration.

The repentance of David became the model of repentance for Jews and Christians.

The New Testament

Paul, the first writer of anything in the New Testament, described the believer's experience with Jesus Christ. He wrote, "We [believers] are buried with him by baptism into death: as Christ was raised from the dead by the glory of the Father, even so, we also should walk in newness of life" (Rom. 6:4, KJV). Because Jesus died and rose again, believers die to their old sin natures and rise to new lives [change] through faith in Christ. Baptism, by immersion, is the acting out of the spiritual experience expressed by Paul.

The author of John's gospel, who wrote about 50 years after Paul, had Jesus say this, "Truly, truly, I say to you, the hour is coming, and now is, when the dead will hear the voice of the Son of God, and they that hear will live" (Jn. 5:25, KJV). At this point in Jesus' dialogue, it is clear he is describing spiritual resurrection from spiritual death—the new birth in the Spirit also described in *John Chapter 3*. Jesus will call his chosen ones from the deadness of their sinful hearts, and they will experience spiritual life. He told Mary, the sister of Lazarus, "those who believe will never die" (John 11:25, KJV).

There is a disconnect between the experience described by *Paul* and *John* and many sincere Christians who don't identify with the born-again phenomenon. They are usually brought up in the faith and in churches practicing infant baptism. No one anticipates a born-again event; only a credible expression (confession) of faith is expected. Many Baptist and independent churches, however, look for the born-again experience in an adult or child before baptizing them.

Considering both Paul and the author of John were proselytizing Gentiles, not Jews, it is understandable they were looking for experiential conversions.

Spiritual Esotericism

After I became an atheist, evangelicals told me I had never truly believed because I never had a relationship with Jesus. For them, something more than believing in Jesus is necessary. A true believer must have a spiritual connection with Jesus. How could they make a judgment about my former faith? Here's how. They cited verses from the Bible, especially two found in I John 2:19-20:

> They [antichrists] went out from us, but they were not of us; for if they had been of us, they would have continued with us. But they went out, that it might become plain that they all are not of us. But you have been anointed by the Holy One, and you all have knowledge." (ESV)

The author makes a clear distinction between true believers (us) and antichrists (them). Within the context of the passage, antichrists are people who turn away from the faith (verse 18), a person like me. In verse 20, the author makes clear that true believers "have the anointing of the Holy One and [therefore] understand everything" (a more literal translation). The word for *know* (*oidate*) may be translated to *understand*. Those who leave the faith never understood it. That is what the author believed, and that is what evangelicals believe because, according to them, it is the Word of God.

I once believed what they did. I knew the Bible that way. I was once blind to the Bible as ancient literature. I had closed my eyes to its humanness and convinced myself it contained a living message from God to me. I believed the Holy Spirit opened the message in my soul so I could understand it and apply it to my life, absorb it into my heart, and make it my experience. That is how I imagined a relationship with Jesus. Of course, I deluded myself by blind faith.

Evangelicals believe: As one cannot understand the Word without the help of a trained teacher, nor can one understand it without the insight given by the Holy Spirit. You cannot really understand the Bible as the Word of God until you are born again by the Holy Spirit. Paul wrote:

> But as it is written, "Eye has not seen, nor ear heard, neither have entered into the heart of man, the things which God has prepared for those who love him [quoting Is.64:4]. But God has revealed them unto us by his Spirit, for the Spirit searches all things, yes, the deep things of God. For what man knows [understands] the things of a man, except the spirit of man which is in him? Even so, no man knows [understands] the things of God except the Spirit of God. Now we have received not the spirit of the world, but the spirit which is of God that we might know [understand] the things that are freely given to us of God. Which things also we [Paul and his companions] speak, not in the words which man's wisdom teaches, but which the Holy Ghost teaches, comparing spiritual things with spiritual. But the natural man does not receive the things of the Spirit of God, for they are foolishness unto him; neither can he know them, because they are spiritually discerned. (I Cor. 2:9-14, MINE)

In the passage above, understanding is *esoteric*. The Holy Spirit imparts understanding so one can believe. The believer's spiritual and

63

mystical union with Jesus Christ results in spiritual *enlightenment,* which alone can unlock the *true* meaning of the Bible.

If you don't understand the message of the Bible, that's because God has chosen not to reveal it to you *by his Spirit.* "And we impart this in words," Paul wrote, "not taught by human wisdom but *taught by the Spirit,* interpreting spiritual truths to those who possess the Spirit." Unbelievers can't understand the Bible with their *natural* [unconverted] *minds.* Reason alone cannot fathom spiritual truths.

However, once you begin to use reason, you will understand the Bible for what it is: a collection of fallible human documents about religion written two to three thousand years ago.

This spiritual insight is the result of being *born again* by the Holy Spirit. *Born-again* language was introduced in the *Gospel According to John* as part of Jesus' dialogue with Nicodemus. "…Unless one is born again," Jesus said, "he cannot *see*[19] the kingdom of God" (John 3:3). Why do we need that kind of spiritual rebirth? Because we all are born spiritually dead, blind to God and his will, and disabled to do any good or even to exercise faith.

If I had real faith, evangelicals insist, I would have never left the faith.

Transcending the Bible

What is the impact of the teaching of esoteric spiritual knowledge in relationship to God and the Bible? The Bible is nothing more than a book with words on paper; however, as evangelicals believe, the enlightenment of the Spirit is vital, personal, and existential. No one can tell the believer what he or she has experienced. No one can deny it. It doesn't matter if the Bible has contradictions and errors because the believer's relationship with Jesus is *absolute* and results in infallible knowledge. The born-again, spiritual experience transforms the obscure

---

[19] The Greek verb *orao* can mean to see, observe, notice, perceive, understand, etc.

64

Bible into the clear Word of God, not unlike breaking a code. Faith brings the Bible to life.

Consequently, the Bible is *secondary*, but the Spirit living in and speaking to the heart is *primary*. The personal revelation of the Holy Spirit (the experience) transcends the Bible.

John's, Freddy's, and my experiences were the real things, from our perspectives. I don't know about them, but my perspective changed.

Chapter 9

The Saved and the Lost

After resigning from the pastorate, I began officiating wedding ceremonies in many different venues. I made it a side-business. One ceremony had Catholic, Christian, Jewish, and Muslim guests. Everybody, including the bride and groom, came from Chicago. The bride and her parents were evangelical. The groom was an unbeliever.

I was meeting the bride's parents for the first time at the rehearsal. They assumed I was a born-again evangelical pastor. As all of us were preparing for the ceremony to begin, the bride's father assured me his family members were all born-again believers.

"David," the father told me in confidence, referring to the groom, "isn't a believer," and added, "but we're praying for him." Said in a manner to convey prayer would take care of the problem. Let me rephrase the typical evangelical perspective: *He isn't one of us yet, but we're praying for him so he will be.* Statements like David's stepfather highlight the distinction evangelicals make between two classes of people—the saved and the lost.

In the previous chapter, we saw in Paul's first letter to the Corinthians his distinction between the *spiritual person* and the *natural person*, exposing the great dichotomy imposed by evangelicals on all people. The spiritual person is enlightened; the natural person is in darkness and ignorant of the truth.

The Jews and the Gentiles

The social dichotomy existed before the New Testament in the form of the Hebrew worldview. Sometime between the eighth to sixth centuries BCE, the prophets began to recognize that Yahweh was not only Israel's God, but he was also the only God. Before then, the Israelites believed there were other gods, but Yahweh was Israel's God, and he was more powerful than all other gods. Statements made by Elijah, King David, and Solomon, who worshipped the gods of his many wives, make this evident.

66

Sometime after the sixth century, the Hebrews believed Yahweh was the only God. Scholars believe the Jews' captivity in Babylon contributed to the belief in pure monotheism. Salvation was about Yahweh saving Israel from her enemies and restoring the nation to the former glory it enjoyed under Solomon's reign. Yahweh would restore an anointed (messiah king), a descendant of David, and his dynasty would last forever. Since Yahweh is the only God, the Gentiles will also find a place in the kingdom of Messiah but in a subservient role. In the Hebrew mind, the division of all people was between Israel and the nations (Goyim), everyone else. For some in the Jewish faith, that division still exists.

Many evangelical Christians continue to believe that the Jewish people continue to be God's chosen people, more special to him than Gentiles ever could be. They believe the return of the Jews to Israel is the fulfillment of prophecy, the precursor to the appearance of the antichrist, followed by the return of Jesus the Messiah. The Jews will then be converted to faith in Jesus as the Messiah. However, the Jews have a different idea while they enjoy the support of evangelicals for Israel as a nation.

The gospels of *Mark* and *Matthew* portray Jesus as the Messiah of the Jewish people as evidenced by Jesus' dialogue with the Syrophoenician woman: "It is not right to take the children's [Jew's] bread and toss it to dogs [Gentiles]" (Mark 7:27, TNIV). In Matthew's account of the same event, Jesus told his disciples, "I was sent only to the lost sheep of Israel (Matt. 15:24, TNIV). When Jesus sent out the 12 disciples to preach repentance to the Jew, he told them, "Do not go among the Gentiles or enter any town of the Samaritans (10:5, TNIV). Jesus maintained the division of humans into *Jews* and *Gentiles*.[20]

The Apostle Paul changed the playing field in two ways. First, every human being on earth is given equal standing before God: everyone (Jew and Gentile alike) is born spiritually dead in trespasses and sins. Everyone is born spiritually lost and will go to hell if not saved by Jesus. Even though the Jews have some advantage because they had

---

[20] I say, "that Jesus" because, as we will see, the Jesus described by Matthew, Mark and Luke is very different from the Jesus described by the author of John's Gospel.

67

God's covenant and the law, the law condemns both Jews and Gentiles as guilty sinners before God. Everyone is born with a spiritual deficit.

Second, salvation is no longer corporate as it was for the Jews as a nation. Salvation is spiritual, personal, and involves the eternal destiny of each soul. Every Jew and every Gentile needs individual salvation from sin and death. That sums up the message of Paul's letter to the Romans. Saved souls comprise the collective church. He erased the division between *Jews* and *Gentiles*.

Presbyterians added a new distinction to the idea of the church. Not everyone, they believe, who claims to be a Christian, is a true believer. The solution? There is a *visible* church—those who claim to be Christian. They make a profession of faith and attend worship services; from every appearance, they are believers. However, some of them are Christian only in name, nominal. Within that group is the *invisible church,* invisible to us because we can't be sure who they are. They are the *real* Christians. Only God knows who they are. But there's more. The *invisible church* is comprised of "the whole number of the elect that has been, are, or shall be gathered into one, under Christ the head thereof..."[21]

To understand this, imagine the church, not as one congregation or even one denomination, but all Christian believers in the world today, add to them all the believers who ever lived (now in heaven) and all the believers who will ever be—like the twinkle in God's eye. For this reason, it is also called the mystical church, or the mystical body of Christ. As God is a timeless being, existing outside and apart from time and space, so is his true church. The invisible church is cosmic—seated in heavenly places in Christ (Eph. 2:6). Yes, it is difficult to understand. These theologians went overboard with philosophy and imagination, blended with physics.

The author of *John's* gospel carried forward the divisive theme of the *saved* and the *lost*. The Jewish people, not the Pharisees, are depicted as the enemies of Jesus. He told the Jewish crowds they could no longer boast about having Abraham as their father. Their father is the

---

[21] Chapter 25:1, *Of the Church*, Westminster Confession of Faith, Edinburg, Scotland, 1647.

Devil (Jn. 8:39-44). Jesus offers eternal life to every person who hears the gospel; it is clear from Jesus' conversation with the Samaritan woman (Jn. 4) and his argument with the Jewish leaders (Jn. 5:16-30).

> Truly, truly, I say to you: he who hears my word and believes on him who sent me has everlasting life and will not come into condemnation but is passed from death to life. Truly, truly, I say to you: the hour is coming, and now is, when the dead will hear the voice of the Son of God, and they who hear will live. For as the Father has life in himself, so has he given to the Son to have life in himself, and has given him authority to execute judgment also, because he is the Son of man. Don't be amazed at this, for the hour is coming in the which all that are in the graves shall hear his voice and will come out; they who have done good to the resurrection of life, and they that have done evil to the resurrection of damnation. (John 5:24-29)

In this passage, we see that Jesus has the power to call individuals to eternal life before they die. Reformed theologians have referred to this as the "effectual call" to salvation. In the last days, he will also have the power to summons each person from the grave. Those who believe in Jesus will join him in heaven; those who reject him will be condemned and destroyed. There are and will forever be the *saved* and the *lost*.

Saving lost souls became my burden as a young pastor, as reflected almost every day in my diary. Out in the small community in which I lived, there were two groups of people, the saved and the lost. The lost were going to hell; it didn't matter how good they were or thought they were. Like everyone else, they, too, were born dead in trespasses and sins. Jesus is the only way to salvation—the way, the truth, and the life, and no one can come to the Father except by him (Jn. 14:6, TNIV).

Theological Problem

What about those who live in places where they never heard about Jesus? As noted earlier, there are very few. The burden of evangelical foreign missions is to take the gospel to those places so the people living there can hear the gospel and be saved. A few places like that still exist.

Within this century, a young missionary was killed attempting to evangelize the indigenous people living on an isolated island for millennia. The nation to which the Island belonged passed a law in the twentieth century prohibiting anyone from coming within miles of the Island. The law was intended to protect the inhabitants from viruses against which they have no immunities, a threat that could wipe out their small population.

The missionary was burdened to bring the gospel message to the Islanders. On his first attempt to come ashore, the natives threatened him and chased him away by throwing spears at his boat. The missionary, however, was undaunted. He returned and landed on shore, where he was killed and buried by the inhabitants. His body cannot be retrieved, nor can any arrest be made because the law protects the indigenous people.

The missionary wasn't to blame. The natives weren't to blame; they warned him, and they were protecting themselves. The teachers at a Christian college taught him to take the gospel to people who never heard it, and a missionary agency trained him to do it. That was the same teaching and training I received at Shelton College. If people hear the saving gospel of God's love through Jesus Christ, they can believe and have an abundant and eternal life. Withholding the gospel is the worst kind of deprivation. Sharing the gospel is the noblest, most selfless act.

There are the *saved,* and there are the *lost*.

Today I enjoy seeing all human beings as equals. The imaginary dichotomy of the *saved and the lost* has vanished from my mind. I love being part of the human family. Each of us is alike in many respects, while each of us is unique. We love each other in the same way with the same emotions. We commit the same sins with the same consequences. We all hurt each other, help each other, and forgive one another. We laugh at the same jokes and cry at the same melodramas. One group of people is not more enlightened or better than another.

Chapter 10

Transcendence

In the iron age, people believed in gods to protect them from drought, famine, blight, and marauders. When gods favored the people, they sent rain, blessed their crops and livestock, and kept warring tribes away. Concerns and needs were mundane and involved survival in a hostile world. The gods exercised ultimate control over the world and the events occurring in it. The solution to human problems came from above—from the gods. People placed their faith, trust, and hope in beings from above.

Transcending Oppression

When the Jews returned to Jerusalem after their captivity in Babylon in 539 BCE, they believed their troubles were over. They would obey God faithfully and worship him only. Ezra, the scribe, returned to Jerusalem shortly after 444 BCE to enforce the law of God and to ensure the priests offered sacrifices in the temple faithfully and maintained the annual feast days. The blessings promised in *Deuteronomy* would be realized—the Jews would keep the land God gave them, and he would bless them in it. They would be free of foreign occupiers. However, things didn't turn out that way. New emerging empires—the Greeks, then the Romans—invaded and subjugated Palestine in turn.

Many Jews began to look beyond national blessings and earthly happiness to a new order and final peace ushered in by the Messiah (Anointed One), a king, the Son of God. Belief in the afterlife and the resurrection of the dead found its way into the Jewish faith. Their enemies may rule them in this life, but in death, their souls would be free. In the resurrection, the Jews would live on the earth again with the Messiah as their king in Jerusalem. By a cataclysmic intervention, Messiah would destroy their enemies and established his kingdom in Jerusalem. The books of *Daniel* and *Enoch* advanced the teaching, and it took hold among many Jewish people in Palestine.

Believers sought to rise above the world with its afflictions—to transcend them. The austere lifestyles of the Essene community established in the mountainous desert near the dead sea reflected the new faith. They recorded their beliefs on scrolls discovered in caves near the dead sea. They are known as the *Dead Sea Scrolls*. Their influence spread beyond their monastic community to cities and towns throughout Palestine.

That was the social, political, and religious world into which John the Baptist and Jesus of Nazareth were born. Their spiritualized and transcendent hopes were evident in their practice of baptism, John's avoidance of the temple, and Jesus' criticism of materialistic practices allowed in the temple. The Essences were so critical of the political and monetary corruption of the priests they refuse to worship there.

Transcending Humanness

The ultimate transcendence, however, was overcoming the weaknesses and vulnerabilities of humanness. It was an endeavor to escape the corruption of the flesh and draw closer to God. Men and women wanted spiritual power to overcome greed, envy, and lust. To do that, they denied the comforts of the flesh and observed strict regimens. They influenced the early Christian monastic movement, whose adherents practiced celibacy and even greater austerity.

Spiritual transcendence continued throughout the history of the church, as evidenced by the ascetic practices of the early stylites, or pillar dwellers. They were holy men who lived for decades on top of forty-foot columns as a means of mortifying the flesh and meditating on God. The columns were built with mortared stones and had a room at the top about six feet square. The stylites hoisted their food and water and lowered their excrement.[22] Others lived in mountain caves as a means of escaping the corruption of the world and drawing nearer to God.

The practice continued in medieval times in monasteries for men and convents for women throughout Europe and the Mediterranean world. Francis of Assisi came from a wealthy Italian family but chose to wander as a poor preacher of the gospel. Many began to follow him. The Pope eventually persuaded him to organize his followers into a holy

---

[22] En.wikipedia.org/wiki/Stylites, March 1212.

72

order of monks who became known as the Franciscans. While committed to a life of poverty, Francis set about to restore ruined churches in the thirteenth century.

Martin Luther joined the Augustinian order and lived in the monastery in Erfurt. From the privacy of his cell, he lashed his back daily with a small whip to overcome lustful thoughts and sensations—the results of human depravity and the corruption of the flesh. Luther ended the practice when he found peace in the teaching of salvation by faith alone. Soon after, the Reformation occurred in 1516 CE. Priest and monks, Luther among them, left the monasteries and married nuns who embraced the new faith and left their convents.

When in Parochial school, our teacher, a nun, told us that Martin Luther started the Reformation because he wanted to get married. I don't believe that was the case, but it sounded like a good enough reason. The struggle with the flesh found its legitimate outlet. He and his wife, Katarina von Bora, had six children.

From what I have seen in my experience, some Evangelicals and Roman Catholics attempt to transcend their humanity. I can confess that it was something I believed in and tried to do. My diary notes are full of references to a tortured soul, unable to transcend the lustful thoughts of the flesh. That a holy God could see my thoughts and would judge me for them was a constant torment. According to some psychologists, men think about sex 8,000 times a day.

The teaching of mortifying the flesh is Biblical, found in the writings of Paul—Romans Chapter 6 through 8, Galatians 5:13-26 and can be summed up in one verse: "Those who belong to Christ have crucified the flesh with the affections and lusts" (Gal. 5:24, KJV). The writings of Paul lead the reader to conclude the struggle ends when believers are spiritually resurrected in their baptisms by faith. However, in real experience, the trouble only begins; prohibitions on imagination, sensations, and feelings only exacerbate them.

From the perspective of the author of Ephesians [not Paul], Christ has resurrected believers from their spiritual death of sinful cravings and desires and given them spiritual life and power. Christ "has raised us [believers] up together and made us sit together in heavenly places in

Christ Jesus" (Eph. 2:6). As we saw in the previous chapter, while believers continue to live on earth, in a cosmic and mystical sense, they are already seated in the presence of Christ in heaven. The way to overcome the flesh is to imagine yourself with Christ.

How many times a day do you think believers imagine themselves sitting in *heavenly place in Christ*? It can assure you it isn't 8,000 times a day.

In *Romans*, Paul teaches perfectionism: upon conversion, believers cease from sin and conduct their lives in holiness by baptism in the Spirit.

Various forms of perfectionism were developed by orthodox theologians throughout church history, beginning with Irenaeus (mid-second century). Some described stages of perfection that would be completed only after death, while others, like John Wesley in the eighteenth century, believed a sinless life was obtainable before death. The teaching disappeared in the mainline Methodist denomination but survived in smaller Methodist offshoots that describe themselves as *holiness* churches with this twist—salvation is lost when the believer sins but can be restored through repentance. The believer can go through an endless cycle of being saved and lost and hopefully will die in the state of salvation.

The Calvinist and Reformed Churches rejected perfectionism and continue to struggle interpreting Romans 6 through 8 and Galatians 5. Their teaching: the believer being "set free from the law of sin and death" is not experiential, but positional in relationship to Jesus.

Either way, spiritual idealism should be recognized in either of those teachings, another example of what makes biblical Christianity unsustainable if not incomprehensible. Both are attempts by Paul and later theologians to transcend humanness. The colleagues I knew all struggled with the passages cited above. All of us read different interpretations, only to be left with nagging questions. If they are the words of God, they must be comprehensible, right? Paul's imagination got the better of him, and it affected every theologian, commentator, and pastor to follow.

Chapter 11

Angels and Demons

Several years ago, a young woman driving her car on a Midwest highway was hit by a drunk driver. The collision was so violent it trapped her in the car. She needed immediate medical care if she was to survive. The fire department and EMTs arrived soon after but didn't have adequate tools to free her. The EMTs began to do everything they could to keep her alive while they waited for the arrival of heavier equipment. Traffic was stopped. People got out of their cars to give assistance or to see what happened; they were taking pictures with their smartphones.

The young woman was conscious enough to ask for prayer. A man appeared, seemingly from nowhere. Dressed as a priest, he applied oil to her head from a small bottle and prayed over her. The prayer calmed her, allowing the EMTs to keep her alive. Minutes later, another truck arrived with equipment to free her from the wreck. She was rushed to the hospital and survived.

But what happened to the man who prayed for her? People said he appeared from nowhere then vanished. Some testified he walked out of the cornfield and disappeared back into it. He never appeared in anyone's pictures. The story spread that he was an angel.

"I think that this time, I've actually witnessed a guardian angel at work," commented one of the firefighters.

In the days following, inquiries were made of churches within a 40-mile radius of the accident if the mystery man was associated with any of them. Nothing. No one came forward. People were convinced the woman's guardian angel appeared and saved her.

Finally, a Roman Catholic priest identified himself as the man in question. He had walked from his stopped car, and after he prayed, he returned to it and waited like everyone else.

I came across many other stories about supposed guardian angels. The stories impressed me because they demonstrate how much people want to believe in angels, the supernatural servants of God, guardians of those assigned to their care, performing acts of kindness, mercy,

76

deliverance, and healing. If a rational answer is not immediately forthcoming, it must be an angel.

We embellish our stories and change them to make them more exciting and unusual, more *newsworthy*. Movie producers call this artistic license, which we all practice. As a pastor, I observed that some foreign missionaries were especially notorious for exaggerating stories of miracles and angelic interventions when they speak to congregations for monetary support.

Biblical Sources

Angel means *messenger,* the messenger of God. Even though the creation of angels is never mentioned in the Bible, theologians have assumed God created them because they believe God created everything. There is no account in the Bible about when he created them, but from the earliest accounts, they seem to have always been with God.

Angels are spirits; however, they can transform themselves into men, or at one time they could, as we will see. When the Sadducees challenged Jesus' Pharisaic belief about the resurrection, he said to them, "You err, not knowing the scriptures, nor the power of God, for in the resurrection they neither marry, nor are given in marriage, but are as the angels of God in heaven" (Matt.22:29:30, KJV). After the resurrection, God's children will have bodies, but they will not engage in sexual intercourse; they will, in some sense, be androgynous; therefore, they will be like the angels—sexless. What about those who are resurrected then sent to hell? Will they be sexless too? The Bible and theologians are silent on that one.

Let's go to the first reference to an angel in the oldest written source of the Hebrew Bible. After Yahweh cursed Adam and Eve for their disobedience, he drove them out of the garden and set a *hakerubim* (cherub) east of the garden to guard the way to the tree of life; ostensibly, to prevent Adam and Eve or any future people from taking the fruit of the tree of life and eating it.

The Serpent

In the Adam and Eve myth, the serpent (snake), known for its subtlety and venom, tempted Eve to eat the forbidden fruit from the tree of the knowledge of good and evil, thereby disobeying the direct prohibition of God. In the traditional interpretation, Satan possessed the snake as a disguise to tempt her. However, there is nothing to support that interpretation. I believe the authors intended the snake to be understood literally. It had legs before it tempted Eve. God judged the snake by removing its legs, condemning the species to crawl on its belly in the dirt. That is why snakes, the ancient enemies of man, have no legs. In *Revelations* 12:9 and 20:2, the author associated Satan with the *old serpent*, a reference to the myth in the Book of Genesis.

Evangelical fundamentalists continue to believe in the historical accuracy of the account—it is the inerrant Word of God. It is the true story of how humans became sinners.

What became of the Garden of Eden? Did it vanish? No one has an answer. Imagine what you like.

The Watchers

Angels do not appear again until Genesis Chapter 6, where they are involved in the reason why Yahweh brought the great flood. Miscreant angels were to blame.

And it came to pass when men began to multiply on the face of the earth, and daughters were born unto them. The sons of God saw the daughters of humans that they were fair, and they took them wives of all which they chose. And Yahweh said, "My spirit will not stay with humankind forever because they are also flesh. Their days [time] will be 120 years.[23] There were giants in the earth in those days, and after that, when the sons of God came in unto the daughters of men, and they bore children to them, the same became mighty men which were of old, men of renown. Gen. 6:1-4. (TNIV)

This passage has confounded pastors, commentators, and theologians for millennia. From the third or second century BCE, the Jews believed the "sons of God" were angels who saw beautiful women and agreed among themselves to take them as their wives and have children with them. This belief may have preceded the third century, but we have no evidence.

---

[23] Meaning is uncertain. Either the flood will come in 120 years, or people will not live beyond 120 years old.

According to the book of *I Enoch*, the angels, identified as watchers, transformed themselves into men. The act of lusting for women and taking them as wives was their great sin, the cause of their fall from heaven.

According to *Enoch*, the angel Semjaza was the leader of 200 Watchers in the days of Jared. They descended upon Mt. Hermon. A nagging question is how beings who are spirits could have lusted after women? The myth is unclear, as myths usually are.

The story is found in the *1st Book of Enoch*, Chapters 6 through 18, written in the second century BCE, but attributed to the patriarch Enoch, the seventh descendant of Adam. The author of *Enoch* wanted to clarify what is otherwise incomprehensible in *Genesis 6:1-4*.

God took Enoch to heaven because he was faithful. He thereby escaped death (Gen. 5:21-24). The only other biblical character to escape death was Elijah, taken up to heaven in a chariot of fire. Where are the bodies of Enoch and Elijah? They're not dead. Ancient Hebrew stories like these suggest the Hebrews, like other peoples in the ancient Mediterranean world, understood heaven to be part of the physical cosmos.

The book was regarded as Scripture by many of the Jewish people before and during the time of Jesus. It was copied and preserved by the Essene community. At least to the end of the second century CE, the Christian community regarded the book as sacred. The Ethiopian Orthodox Church and the Eritrean Orthodox Church included *Enoch* in the Old Testament Canon.

The New Testament author, Jude, made a direct reference to *Enoch*: "The angels who did not keep their first estate, but left their habitation, he [God] has reserved in everlasting chains under darkness unto the judgment of the great day" (Jude 6, KJV). Jude's reference is to *Enoch 10:12, 13*: "When their sons have slain one another, and they have seen the destruction of their beloved ones, bind them fast [God commands the angels] for seventy generations under the hills of the earth until the day of the consummation of their judgment and until the eternal judgment is accomplished. In those days they shall be led off to the abyss of fire and to the torment and the prison in which they shall be confined forever." *Jude* identifies the *Prophecy of Enoch* in verse 14.

The author of 2 Peter also referenced the legend of the Watchers: "God did not spare angels when they sinned, but sent them to hell [Tartarus], putting them in chains of darkness to be held for judgment" (2 Pe. 2:4).

Then who are the demons that roam the earth today, according to the Bible? The author of *Enoch* provided an explanation. The evil spirits (demons) who torment humans are the spirits of the children of the *Watchers*. Their children were the *Giants, the Nephilim* (Genesis. Chapter 6). Before the righteous angels bound the Watchers under the hills, the Watchers witnessed "the destruction of their loved ones." What was their destruction? The Nephilim killed each other.

8. And now, the giants, who are produced from the spirits [Watchers] and flesh [women], shall be called evil spirits on the earth,

9. And shall live on the earth. Evil spirits have come out from their bodies because they are born from humans and from holy Watchers, their beginning is of primal origin;

10. They shall be evil spirits on earth, and evil spirits they shall be called, spirits of the evil ones. (As for the spirits of heaven [angels], in heaven shall be their dwelling, but as for the spirits of the earth which were born on the earth, on the earth shall be their dwelling.) And the spirits of the giants afflict, oppress, attack, war, destroy, and cause trouble on the earth. (Enoch 15:8-10)

While the holy angels live in heaven and the spirits of the giants (Nephilim) or demons live on the earth where they afflict humans. These are the same demons who tormented people with physical and mental illnesses in Jesus' time. They are the same demons, a legion of them, whom Jesus cast out of the man who lived among the tombs in Gergesa (Matt. 8:28-34). The demons cried out to Jesus, "Have you come here to torture us before the appointed time?"

What is the appointed time? The end of time, the consummation of the age when the bodies of the giants will be resurrected, united with their spirits, and cast into the burning fire forever (Enoch 16:1).

What about Lucifer?

The name *Lucifer, Morning Star,* is found in the King James translation of Isaiah 14:12. However, the Hebrew name for *Morning Star* is *helel.* We know the *Morning Star* as the planet *Venus*, the Roman name for the female goddess. In the ancient Mediterranean and Middle Eastern cultures, a myth existed about the planet Venus. It was a lesser god who attempted to rise and exult itself among the greater gods (stars) higher in the night sky. However, the gods cast it down to the horizon. In the Babylonian myth, *the morning star* is *Etana* (male). In the Isaiah passage, the prophet compares Nebuchadnezzar's demise, the king of Babylon and Israel's nemesis, to that of the morning star, *Etana.* As the god, Etana attempted to exalt himself but was cast down by the other gods, so Nebuchadnezzar, who oppressed God's people, will be cast down to the grave in shame.

The passage has nothing to do with the devil.

The name *Lucifer* is the Latin word for *morning star.* The title is found in the Latin translation of the Bible from the fourth century (the Vulgate). The King James translators retained the Latin word because the passage in Isaiah Chapter 14 was believed to describe the devil.

The Roles of Angels

To review the roles of angels in the entire Bible would require volumes. Here are some of those roles:

1. They are Divine messengers and deliverers (Gen. 19). They delivered Lot and his family. One special angel guided and protected the Hebrews and destroyed their enemies (Ex. 23:20-24).

2. An angel exhorted the Hebrews and chided them for not driving out the indigenous people of Canaan (Deut. 2:15). In this unique role, the angel took the place of Yahweh or a prophet.

3. Warriors: Before Joshua attacked Jericho, he was met by an angel who identified itself as the "commander of the army of Yahweh" (Joshua 5:14). Angels appeared as the army of Yahweh in 2 Kings 6:17 when the King of Syria sent soldiers to arrest Elisha, who made this prayer for his frightened servant: "'Open his eyes, Yahweh, so that he may see.' Yahweh opened the servant's eyes, and he looked and saw the hill full of chariots of fire all around Elisha."

Stories about angels as the army of Yahweh would become popular in Palestine among the Jews beginning in the second century BCE and to the Christians in the first and second centuries CE. The author of *Enoch* may have been the first to describe the angelic army of God as comprising hundreds of thousands. "And after that, I saw thousands of thousands and ten thousand times ten thousand" (Enoch 40:1).

The same vision of the massive army of angels is found again in Daniel 7:10: "A river was flowing out from before him (The Ancient of Days). Thousands upon thousands attended him; ten thousand times ten thousand stood before him." The author of *Jude* quoted *Enoch* 40:1. "Enoch, the seventh from Adam, prophesied about them: 'See, the Lord is coming with thousands upon thousands of his holy ones to judge everyone, and to convict all of them of all the ungodly acts they have committed in their ungodliness, and of all the defiant words ungodly sinners have spoken against him'" (Jude 14-15 NIV).

This apocalyptic device reached its zenith in the *Apocalypse of John* (The Book of Revelation). At the end of days, the rider on the white horse who is called faithful and true, on whose head are many crowns, whose robe is dipped in blood and "whose name is the Word of God" is followed by the army of heaven, riding on white horses. The rider on the white horse is Jesus Christ; together with his army, he will destroy "the Beast" and the kings who follow him (Rev. 19:11-21).

Guardian Angels

There isn't much biblical information about guardian angels. Something in Acts 12:15 may suggest a belief in guardian angels in Jesus' time. When the Apostle Peter was arrested and jailed, he was set free with the help of an angel. When he came to the house of John Mark's mother and asked to be let in, a servant named Rhoda recognized Peter's voice, but those who were in the house said in objection, "It must be his angel" (NIV). The meaning is not clear. While this statement reflects first-century superstitions in Palestine, it isn't strong evidence for the belief in guardian angels. Their supposed existence we must leave to the collective Christian imagination over the centuries, the desire to believe we each have a guardian angel to help and protect us. It raises the question: does God create new angels to keep up with population growth?

A Christian woman told a group of us at a social event how she was struggling with her luggage in the airport when two young men *appeared from nowhere* on either side of her and asked if they could carry her luggage. She accepted their help gladly. When she arrived at the gate, they seemed to *disappear*. "I know they were angels sent by God to help me," She said. I don't think so. They were simply two nice young men who hurried on their way.

Chapter 12
Heaven and Hell

Neither the teachings of Christian churches nor the Bible presents explicit descriptions of heaven or hell. What we can glean from the Bible and other ancient texts and myths is that heaven and hell are part of the material world. Heaven is in the expanse above the earth, up there somewhere. Hell is beneath the earth's surface. Modern understanding of geology, astronomy, and physics has dispelled those ideas. Pastors I have known believe both places exist in an invisible, spiritual realm undetected by modern science. What other choice do they have?

Heaven

Heaven is the home of God and his angels. In the Hebrew Bible, angels are depicted as praising God in heaven and serving him in various ways on earth among humans. They are messengers and sometimes interfere in the natural order of the cosmos.

Most Christians believe the souls of believers go to heaven, consciously enjoying the presence of God. These souls await the resurrection of the dead when God reunites their bodies with their souls. However, the Jehovah's Witnesses and the Seventh Day Adventists believe in soul sleep, i.e., the souls of believers after death are not conscious but sleep until the day of resurrection. There was a man in one of the congregation I pastored who believed in soul sleep. He won me over, but I regarded the question too obscure and unimportant. By that time, I realized many traditional teachings were not crucial enough for an argument.

You can find verses in the Bible to support both views, which is true of so many trivial theological disputes hotly contested.

Hell

As we saw from *Enoch*, the *Watchers* are bound in the abyss, hell. In the *Book of Revelation* (20:1-5), an angel comes down from heaven with a key to the abyss. He binds Satan for a thousand years, the same period in which Christ will rule on earth after his return. After the thousand years, Satan is released for a short time to lead unbelieving nations in a final war against Christ in Jerusalem. There are several interpretations of the confusing accounts in *Revelation*, but I don't want to get into them. The abyss, however, is not depicted as the home of demons. Demons live on earth, as we saw in the previous chapter.

Mythological Sources

The English word for hell comes from Nordic mythology. Hele is the realm of the dead, ruled by the goddess Hela.

The ancient Hebrew teaching about heaven and hell is vague. As late as the time of King Hezekiah and the prophet Isaiah, about 700 BCE, there is no evidence the Hebrews believed in the existence of the devil, life after death, or hell. They believed heaven was the home of God and his angels but not the eternal destination of righteous human beings. God's reward for obedience was prosperity, peace, long life, and an honorable burial. Everyone will die and go into Sheol, the shadowy underworld, translated as *the grave*. "The dead praise not Jehovah, neither any that go down into silence" (Ps. 115:17, KJV). "Shall the dead arise and praise you?" (Ps. 88:10, KJV). The question is rhetorical. They will not.

You cannot find a single reference to anyone living after death in the five books of Moses or the histories. In 1 Samuel Chapter 28, the witch of Endor conjured up the ghost of Samuel, who came *up out of the earth*. Samuel complained to Saul, "Why did you disturb my sleep." When David's infant son died, he said, "He cannot come to me, but I will go to him." It's not clear if David meant anything more than, "I will join him in the royal sepulcher." Passages in the Old Testament seem to contradict each other; some indicate there isn't any life after death or that the dead sleep.

The prophets developed a concept of the resurrection of the dead much later in Israel's history:

Your dead men will live, together with my dead body will they arise. Awake and sing, you that dwell in dust: for your dew is as the dew of herbs, and the earth will cast out the dead. (Is. 26:19, KJV).

The passage cited above, however, is part of a larger section (Chapters 24-27) identified by critical scholars as the *Apocalypse of Isaiah,* written after the Babylonian Captivity or as late as the Greek occupation of Palestine, which would place its composition later than 322 BCE.[24]

The Book of Job contains a reference to the resurrection of the dead:

> For I know that my redeemer lives, and that he will stand at the latter day upon the earth: And though after my skin worms destroy this body, yet in my flesh will I see God: Whom I will see for myself, and my eyes will behold, and not another; though my reins be consumed within me. (Job 19:25-27, KJV).

I used this passage of Scripture at every funeral service. The date of writing is unknown, but many favor a later date in the Hellenist period.

The last reference to the resurrection of the dead in the Old Testament is in the Book of Daniel, written between 150 and 100 BCE, several centuries after Daniel's time. The book appears to be the work of two or more authors.

> And many of them that sleep in the dust of the earth shall awake, some to everlasting life, and some to shame and everlasting contempt. (Daniel 12:2, KJV)

The Jesus described by the author of John's gospel promises believers that after he raises them from the dead, he will take them to rooms prepared for them in his father's house.

> My Father's house has many rooms; if that were not so, would I have told you that I am going there to prepare a place for you? And if I go and prepare a place for you, I will come back and take you to be with me that you also may be where I am. You know the way to the place where I am going. (John 14:2-4 (NIV)

In *Enoch* Chapters 89-90, we find the allegory of the faithful and unfaithful sheep, shepherds, and the second great house the Lord of the sheep built for them. The greater and more beautiful house may be Israel, restored to a greater glory or, it may be symbolic for the new heavens and the new earth.

---

[24] Otto Kaiser, *Isaiah 13-39: A Commentary*, trans. R.A. Wilson (London, SCM Press Ltd., 1974) 173.

And all that had been destroyed and dispersed, and all the beasts of the field, and all the birds of heaven, assembled in that house, and the Lord of the sheep rejoiced with great joy because they were all good and had returned to His house. Enoch 90:33

When *John* was written (about 110 CE), the *1ˢᵗ Book of Enoch* was enjoying its heyday in the Christian community.

The Jesus of the Synoptic Gospels has the kingdom (heaven) on earth, with Jerusalem as its capital. The Book of Revelation also describes heaven on earth; it will begin with a thousand-year reign of Christ on earth, after which Satan will be released from the abyss (hell) and attempt to overthrow Christ. Satan will fail and be bound in hell again. Heaven will then resume on earth. "Then I [John] saw a new heaven and a new earth, for the first heaven and the first earth had passed away, and there was no longer any sea" (Rev. 21:1). In the last chapter, something like the Garden of Eden is restored for all eternity.

What will the saved be doing in heaven? Ask any Christian, and each answer will be different. Because the souls of departed saints are depicted in *Revelations* 7:14-17 as constantly praising God in his presence, many believe that is what they will be doing for eternity. I could see myself getting tired of that quickly, so I rejected that idea. I could see God also getting tired of it. As mentioned earlier, many Christian see heaven as a family reunion.

Heaven can be whatever you want to imagine.

Getting Back to Hell

Nor did the ancient Hebrews have a concept of hell. The prophets made no mention of it. The judgment of God was never described as eternal suffering; rather, judgments were pronounced as warfare, defeat, famine, pestilence, expulsion from the land, an untimely and a disgraceful death without a proper burial.[25]

The prophet Isaiah was thought to refer to hell when he described the death of King Nebuchadnezzar of Babylon, the arch-enemy of Judah— "Yet you will be brought down to *hell*, to the sides of the pit"

---

[25] See the death of Jezebel in 2 Kings 9:30-37. Proverbs 20:17: "Food gained by fraud tastes sweet, but one ends up with a mouth full of gravel."

(Is. 14:15).[26] However, the Hebrew word is *bur* (the *crypt or grave)* and was translated into Greek as *Hades*, the world of the afterlife.

Later Jewish belief in hell may have been derived from the Persian belief in an abyss and the Greek belief in Tartarus, the place to which the wicked were condemned, a hopeless existence of suffering and frustration. The Persians maintained control over Palestine from 539 BCE to their defeat by the Greeks in 332. While some Jews returned to Jerusalem to rebuild the temple (the 2nd Temple period), many, perhaps most, remained in Babylon, Susa (the sometime capital of Persia), and other Persian controlled cities.

The Greeks maintained control over Palestine and Syria for 164 years, first under the Empire of the Greek Ptolemies in Egypt and then by the Greek Seleucid kings of Syria. The syncretism of religious beliefs was inevitable, and it is evident.

Tartarus

The Greeks believed the world is divided into three regions: the surface of the earth on which humans live, the realm above ground, which includes the dome of heaven where Zeus and many gods dwell on Mt. Olympus, and the realm below the earth, the realm of the dead, ruled by Hades and other gods like Tartarus.

The names of the gods became the names of their domains— Hades was also the name of the underworld, Tartarus (hell) named after its god, the realm of tormented souls who had been judged as wicked in their lives.

The souls of the dead descended into Hades and found themselves on the shores of the river Acheron,[27] which they had to cross using the services of Charon, the ferryman to whom they paid a small coin, the obolus, placed in their mouths at burial. Having crossed the Acheron, they made their way to the palace of Hades and stood before three judges—Minos, Rhadamanthus, and Aegeus. The judges sent the righteous and heroes to the blessed Isle of Elysium, but condemned the wicked to Tartarus where they were imprisoned and tormented, a place

---

[26] Prophecies directed against Babylon were written after Cyrus, King of Persia, defeated the Babylonians in 539 BCE and then inserted into the ongoing compilation of Isaiah's Prophecy. More about that later.

[27] Roman: The River Styx.

of gloom and darkness, a place as far below Hades as the earth is below the heavens, as Homer wrote, "...the lowest abyss beneath the earth."[28]

Tartarus was also part of the natural order of the earth; many rivers merged and mixed, reaching the surface as marshes, springs, and lakes. There were also rivers of mud and—more pertinent to our discussion—rivers of fire, the same that flowed from the many volcanoes that erupted on the Greek islands. Palestine had no active volcano for 50,000 years—Mt. Bental in the Golan Heights. That may be why the idea of a fiery hell is not original to the Hebrews or Canaanites.

The Greek belief about Tartarus was easily incorporated into the Jewish faith. The Pharisees accepted the existence of a fiery hell. The Sadducees, however, frowned on the idea of hell as a superstitious belief. Pharisaical ideas about hell were passed onto the Christian Jewish community. Though Jesus avoided labels, he derived his beliefs from the Pharisees and the puritanical sect known as the Essenes, who also believed in hell.

The writer of 2 Peter used the word *Tartarus* as the place of torment for the *angels who sinned* (2 Peter 2:4). The word was translated into English as *hell*.

Gehenna

Gehenna was the Hebrew and Aramaic name for hell, the mysterious realm where the souls of the wicked will be tormented after death. It was also a place outside the walls of Jerusalem—the valley of the Son of Hinnom—where, according to tradition, the idolatrous people of Israel offered their children as living burnt sacrifices on the arms of the idol god, Moloch. The Jews also believed it was the actual entrance to hell.

Isaiah concludes with a final pronouncement of judgment against those who have transgressed against Yahweh— "And they shall go forth and look upon the carcasses of the men that have transgressed against me: *for their worm shall not die, neither shall their fire be quenched*; and they shall be an abhorring unto all flesh" (Isaiah 66:24). The writer was

---

[28] Plato, Phaedo [111c The hollows of the earth]. Socrates' dialogue with Phaedo. "...and there is much fire, and great rivers of fire..."

referring to *Gehenna*, the smoldering rubbish heap outside the city walls of Jerusalem, meaning they would be thrown out with the trash.

Mark's gospel recorded Jesus' words about *hell* (*Gehenna*) clearly as a place of the fiery and everlasting punishment of the wicked. "And if your eye offends you, pluck it out," Jesus said, "it is better for you to enter into the kingdom of God with one eye than having two eyes to be cast into *hell* fire (Gehenna)," Jesus added, quoting the passage above in Isaiah, *"Where their worm dies not, and the fire is not quenched"* (Mk. 9:47-48).

The Jewish rabbis recognized in Isaiah 31:9 a reference to Gehenna— "whose [Yahweh's] fire is in Zion, and his furnace in Jerusalem."[29] That is an interpretation that does not seem to fit the context. The Jewish rabbis, whose teachings later rabbis recorded in the Talmud (the commentaries and sayings), made many references to Gehenna as a hell of torment more frightening than Tartarus.

The author of the Book of Enoch clearly described Gehenna:

And all the idols of the heathen shall be abandoned. And the temples burned with fire, and they shall remove them from the whole earth, and the heathen shall be cast into the judgment of fire and shall perish in the wrath and in grievous judgment forever. *Enoch* 91:9

Heaven and hell are the most riveting creations of ancient human imagination, designed to promise immortality and bliss to the departed who were faithful to God in this life but intended to strike fear in the hearts of the wicked that they might repent before being cast into the eternal flames of torment.

Evangelical Hell

As we saw in Chapter 6, *Can All Those People Be Wrong*, many modern evangelicals have become slicker at marketing Jesus. *Don't talk about hell, but if you do, modify the description into something* less horrible.

---

[29] The school of Rabbi Ishmael teaches that the "fire in Zion" is hell, and "His furnace in Jerusalem" is the gate of hell. Preface to The Talmud, translated by Joseph Barclay, LLD, 1878, Kindle edition, published by Evinity Publishing Inc., 2009, location 473.

Two journalists interviewed the Rev. Billy Graham for a Time Magazine article in 1993. When they asked about hell, he said this:

"The only thing I can say for sure is that hell means separation from God...That is going to be hell. When it comes to a literal fire, I don't preach it because I'm not sure about it...not fire but something worse, a thirst for God that cannot be quenched."[30]

Viewing his sermons on YouTube as far back as 1976, his interpretation of hell was consistent, predicated on his belief that people thirst for God spiritually. He based it on the words of Jesus to the woman at the well of Samaria. Jesus said, "Everyone who drinks this water [well water] will be thirsty again, but whoever drinks the water I give them will never thirst. Indeed, the water I give them will become in them a spring of water welling up to eternal life" (John 4:13-14, NIV). The image is also found in several Psalms (*thirsting after God*). (See also the parable of *The Rich Man and Lazarus*—Luke 16:19-31).

Thirst for something or someone is a metaphor of *desire*—the message: people desire God even though they don't realize it. Hell is the eternal deprivation of any satisfaction, an eternity of despair.

A departure from earlier evangelical interpretations of hellfire as literal, many modern evangelicals have adopted the metaphorical description of hell. It is less offensive than eternal flames that burn painfully but never consume. The Pharisees and Jesus believed in a literal fiery hell, and so did the Christian Church for most of its history. There are enough fundamentalists who continue to believe in and preach literal hellfire.

---

[30] Nancy Gibbs and Richard N Ostling, *God's Billy Pulpit*, Time Magazine, November 15, 1993: 74

Chapter 13

The Power of Prayer

Prayer is talking to God verbally or in thought. Through prayer, one can praise and thank God, request personal help, and make requests for others. Some religions and some Christians recite rote prayers. As a Catholic, I was taught to pray the "Hail Mary" and the "Our Father" (Lord's Prayer) using the rosary. I learned to recite them quickly, as do all Catholic children. They were assigned to me by the priest as penance. "Pray 10 *Our Fathers* and 20 *Hail Marys*," the priest would say after he pronounced absolution. It's hard to remember now, but I think he told me to pray in the hundreds. Now that's ridiculous. I don't think I ever got beyond 10. That was hard enough.

The Amish thank God for their meal after they eat. Most Christians thank God before they eat. I discouraged prayer before public meals, as in a restaurant, because I thought it was contrary to what Jesus taught his disciples: "And when you pray, do not be like the hypocrites, for they love to pray standing in the synagogues and on the street corners to be seen by others… but when you pray, go into your room, close your door…" (Matt. 6:5-6 TNIV). Everyone has heard the evangelical in the restaurant give thanks loudly so everyone can hear. Evangelicals call that a *testimony to their faith*—maybe somebody who hears will get saved. I call it *annoying everyone in the restaurant*.

Biblical Sources for Prayer

The Lord's prayer, found in Matthew 6:9-13 and Luke 11:2-4, is part of the Sermon on the Mount when Jesus taught the multitudes, and in response to the disciples asking him, "Lord, teach us to pray, as John [the Baptist] taught his disciples" (NIV).

Matthew 6:9-13:
Our Father in heaven,
Holy is your name.
Your Kingdom come,
Your will be done.
On earth as in heaven.
Give us our daily bread.

Cancel our debts,
As we forgive our debtors,
And do not lead us into testing (trials),
But deliver us from evil.

Luke 11:2-4:
Father, holy is your name.
Your kingdom come.
Give us our daily bread,
And forgive us our sins,
As we forgive all our debtors.

There are more variant readings in *Luke*. The traditional phrase—*yours be the kingdom, the power, and the glory forever, amen*—is not found in any manuscripts and is usually omitted in modern translations.

The Lord's prayer provides an outline for prayer. However, it found its way into the liturgies of many traditional churches whose congregations recite it in unison to this day. Many evangelicals have dropped it from assemblies because it is liturgical. *Liturgy* is a dirty word among evangelicals because it's too stodgy and ritualistic. Everything in their assemblies today is about upbeat joy, feelings, and relationships—a good thing.

Abraham offered the earliest prayers recorded from whom we hear praise, thanksgiving, and petition. The theme continues throughout the Old Testament. When we arrive at King David's time, we hear his appeals for deliverance from his enemies, his praise that Yahweh is his rock and his strength. Yahweh heard David's confession of sin, in which we recognize his self-denigration as a depraved sinner and his petition for pardon (Psalm 32 and 51).

Evangelical Fundamentalist Prayers Today

Gone are the days when Puritans spent hours in prayer, lamenting they were not on their knees before the rooster crowed or they heard the blacksmith's hammer. Prayer has lost its pietism.

I have attended many prayer meetings in my lifetime. Each sentence of prayer began with, "Father, God, Lord Jesus" or "Jesus wejus." It grates on the ear after a while. Some people didn't know when to quit praying. I would sit there with my eyes closed and my head bowed, thinking, *Please stop.*

Most evangelicals today offer prayers for someone suffering from a chronic illness, about to have surgery, in the hospital, or near death. They pray for the safety of older children who have moved from home, joined the military, are overseas, or on their way back. They pray for the success of meaningful and important life events. They are positive thoughts going out for all kinds of people. However, the greatest benefit of prayer is for the person who prays. Prayer is an expression of personal affirmation, intention, and goodwill.

People also offer prayers for petty and ridiculous things. When I was still in college and attending church, a female member told us how she was asking the Lord to give her a Persian rug. I recently read an article from a Christian author who shared that he prayed for a free trip to Acapulco for his wedding anniversary. After months of praying, God granted his request. He called it a *God-size miracle* because only God can do that. Prayer can be selfish.

Petitions for healing are the most common while the least noted in the Bible. King Hezekiah of Judah prayed for his healing from a deadly disease (Isaiah 38 and 2 Kings 20). The prophet Isaiah came to him and said, "Put your house in order because you are going to die; you will not recover" (Is. 38:1). Hezekiah petitioned the Lord to spare his life. He wept bitterly. Yahweh heard his prayer and sent Isaiah with good news. Yahweh would extend his life for 15 years. It must have been an anxious fifteenth year.

In the New Testament, James, the brother of the Lord, wrote in his epistle, "If anyone is sick, they should call for the elders of the church to anoint the infirmed with oil in the name of the Lord and pray over them, and the prayer offered in faith will make them well" (5:14, KJV). No one knows what "anointing with oil" does or should do. Some commentators explained it away as an antiquated belief. Olive oil, the ancients believed, had medicinal value, not unlike saying, "Have the elders come together to pray for the ill person then give him or her an aspirin." Very few pastors in my evangelical circles cared for that interpretation, but few observed the ritual. It was suspicious. They dropped the practice, but the problem remained: How do you ignore a biblical prescription?

In one of my congregations, the elders and I decided it was a matter of biblical obedience to perform the ritual. An elderly female suffered from undiagnosed abdominal pain. We all agreed to arrive at her house at 7 pm. It was late fall and already dark outside. We had no playbook, so we decided on a plan.

"I suggest we tell her what we are doing and why then read the passage from James 5:14," I said, "then I will anoint her with oil on the forehead. Then each of us can pray for her healing, and I'll close."

No one else had a plan, so they all agreed.

When we arrived, her husband opened the door and welcomed us in. He shook everyone's hand with a smile. There was some small talk. Then he led us to his wife, seated in her armchair in the living room. It was dark. A lamp on a side table spread light down and across the carpet.

The ritual unfolded smoothly. After I applied the oil to her forehead, I handed her a tissue to wipe the oil before it ran down her nose. She was better the next day and at church on Sunday. I felt awkward about the whole thing and never did it again. I think she would have felt better, with or without the ritual. But who knows? Prayer can have a psychological effect on recipients, so can rituals.

A young girl came down with an inexplicable illness that put her in the hospital. She was there for a week. Prayers were offered for her daily through the telephone prayer-chain. That was before people texted. Although she underwent medical tests to discover the cause of her illness, doctors found none. I decided to go to the hospital when the girl's parents were there, and I offered to pray for her. I believed what I was doing was effective. The next morning, she was well and returned home that day.

Lord, What Shall I Do?

Christians offer petitions to "know God's will." (This topic will overlap with the next chapter in which I explore the meaning of God's will). "Lord, show me what you want me to do?" They want to know if they should buy a used car, take a new job, or move to another city. They believe God will *show* them what to do for big and little decisions, and they won't make it until he shows them, somehow.

When I started selling insurance, I got a lead on a man who was interested in buying a small amount of life insurance for his father. After I provided the quote, he hemmed and hawed, asked a few questions, then said, "I'll pray about it." That was the end of the conversation. When I followed up a week later, he asked the same questions, hesitated, and said again, "I'll pray about it."

There was nothing to pray about. He either wanted the insurance or didn't. He could afford it, or he couldn't. He could have said, "If I decide I want it, I'll give you a call." That's how you keep a salesperson from calling you back. I don't believe he ever prayed about it. That is his pat answer when he can't decide or the way he says no. I never called him again, and he never called me.

How God shows anyone his will is never clear—a sign, some serendipitous event. Ultimately, you must decide like everyone else. I would often say to people, "Make your decision based on your experience, judgment, and wisdom. Use what God has given you. Ask friends for advice, but don't expect God to help you make everyday decisions that everyone makes. Ask yourself, "is it right or wrong. Will it hurt me or help me? Will it help or hurt the ones I love? Can the decision be postponed?"

The Positive Power of Prayer

There is an unmistakable psychological power in prayer. Faith in a God who loves you and is all-powerful can empower you with confidence and determination. You've made your decision to take some action, to accomplish something difficult and, yet, rewarding. You believe it's right, and you ask God for the strength to do it. You ask him to go before you and prepare the way. You ask for success, and, *by God*, you pull it off. You succeed. In this way, prayer is like giving yourself a pep talk. As King David wrote:

> With your help, I can advance against a troop; with my God, I can scale a wall… For who is God besides the LORD? And who is the Rock except our God? It is God who arms me with strength and keeps my way secure. He makes my feet like the feet of a deer; he causes me to stand on the heights. He trains my hands for battle; my arms can bend a bow of bronze. You make your saving help my shield, and your right hand sustains me; your help has made me great. You provide a broad path for my feet so that my ankles do not give way. Psalm 18:29, 31-36 (NIV)

David believed God would give him the strength to overcome his enemies. God would go before him to prepare the way, to lay the groundwork. If you make that kind of prayer, you are going to be successful—many failures notwithstanding.

I have done different kinds of jobs in my life, but the toughest job I had was being a pastor. I made important decisions daily that affected my family and the church. I often found myself making prayers like David, petitioning God for his grace and strength. That frame of mind is a potent source of strength and a positive and assertive approach to any task. Anyone can have it, but you must believe it. You must believe in yourself and, if you like, a powerful helper. I have heard people talk about praying to the Universe. Why not? There is a mysterious power there.

I believe that what happened in my life is that I eventually began to believe in myself more as I let go of the myth of God.

Up

Across the board, Christians believe God is everywhere at the same time. Theologians call it the omnipresence presence of God, *omni* meaning *universal*. God is next to you and even inside of you; he is also in hell, though not suffering it, just present. He is present throughout the universe, in everyone one of an infinite number of stars and galaxies. At the same time, traditional Christians believe he is distinct from his creation; he is not part of it. Nonetheless, because of Biblical imagery, Christians close their eyes to pray and imagine a white-bearded Zeus-like figure seated on a throne somewhere up there with Jesus sitting at his right hand.

Why do believers close their eyes when they pray? It is neither a biblical nor church rule. Perhaps because keeping your eyes open may distract you from concentrating on your prayers or Jesus. Looking at something in front of you is failing to experience transcendence. If Jesus is everywhere at the same time in the spirit, he's next to you on the couch; however, sitting on the couch and talking to Jesus next to you doesn't seem right. Better to close your eyes and imagine what you like.

Chapter 14

The Will of God

I alluded to the will of God in the previous chapter. However, what is the *will of God*? What definition can we derive from the Bible? How do evangelicals and other Christians understand the *will of God*, and how do they use the phrase.

Early in his ministry, Jesus entered a house in Galilee. A large crowd gathered outside, seeking him. He had quickly established a reputation as a healer and exorcist. He must have been near Nazareth because his mother and brothers, when they heard about this, went to take him by force, for they believed he was "out of his mind."[31] Someone informed him that his mother and brothers were outside, asking for him, but Jesus wouldn't surrender himself to them.

He looked around at those in the house and said to them, "Here are my mother and my brothers! Whoever does God's will is my brother and sister and mother" (Mark 3:34,35, NIV). The message is clear: those who do what God wants are his family. Doing God's will is obeying his law.

Having attended Shelton College months after my conversion, I learned its theology. My professors defined the *will of God* as the *law of God*. The law of God includes any and all commandments found in the Bible, the gospel accounts, or in the letters of the New Testament. However, that is not the only way the will of God is understood.

The Center of God's Will

Religious definitions change as religion evolves. Popular preachers emerged throughout history who added their interpretive perspectives. Evangelicals in the mid-20th century revered American

---

[31] The incident with Mary and his brothers is found only in Mark's account, the earliest one which portrays a human Jesus. Later writers may have omitted it because the church was leaning toward a divine Jesus as we find him in John's account. The incident may have been genuine. It raises questions about Jesus' mental stability. Was it a family intervention oft repeated? Many details about the historical Jesus are left out that might depict him negatively.

and British evangelists of the late 19th century—male and female preachers and writers who were the founders of fundamentalism. I don't know who began talking about "being in the center of God's will," but it was probably someone from that period. It caught on, big time.

I've always been analytical in my approach to information. The expression caught my attention, and I mauled it over for a long time. Yes. I brainwashed myself, but I was not a zombie. At Shelton College, we had chapel every day at 11:30 before lunch. Once or twice a week, a special guest delivered a 20-minute message after we sang a few hymns. I noticed guest missionaries, home from the field, often used the expression, "the center of God's will."

"You can follow the will of God," the guest speaker said, but looking students in the eye, he or she would ask theatrically, "but are you in the center of God's will?" Then the speaker would pause, letting the question settle on our hearts and minds before uncovering some deep and mysterious truth. I pondered, "Am I in the center of God's will? How could I know? What is the center of God's will?"

It was explained a bit differently each time. Essentially it meant are you exactly where God wants you to be? Are you doing what God wants YOU to do? *Are you preparing for the calling God wants for you?*

I realized over time that it had to do with one's "calling." What is a calling? People—evangelicals and others—would say to me about being a pastor, "What you do is a calling, not a profession." *Excuse me*, I would think to myself. *I am a professional; I make a living doing this.* So, yes. What I do is a calling, but it's also a profession. When doctors earned a lot less money—like when I was a kid—their practice was a calling too.

A calling is doing full-time work for the Lord or for the welfare of humanity. Being a pastor—especially being a missionary—is being in the center of God's will. Nonsense.

Being in the center of God's will was also expressed as being in the closest possible spiritual relationship with God, like Enoch in the OT who "walked with God"—always in prayer and ever submissive. Pious. If you are in the center of God's will, you are invincible. The devil cannot touch you. You are an upper-class Christian spiritually, not just an ordinary Christian.

The Sovereign Will of God

There is another way some evangelicals understand the will of God. His will is his fixed plan for humans and the natural events which will impact them—when, where, and how he has determined. This concept of divine determinism is found in both the Hebrew and Christian Bibles.

When the patriarch Joseph—who was second in command of all Egypt after Pharaoh—revealed himself to his brothers, they were afraid he would take vengeance on them for selling him into slavery (Genesis Chapter 45). However, Joseph assured them he would not do that because it was all part of God's plan to save them from famine. "Don't be distressed, and don't be angry with yourselves," he said to them, "God sent me ahead of you to preserve you and our descendants" (Gen. 45:5, My Paraphrase). Even though his brothers intended to get rid of him, God's plan overshadowed theirs. He used them and their sin to execute his plan.

The author of *Acts of the Apostles* has Peter saying the same thing to the Jews who were responsible for crucifying Jesus. "With the help of wicked men, you put him to death," he told them, "but the man [Jesus] was handed over to you by God's deliberate plan and foreknowledge" (Acts 2:23, NIV). Yes, wicked men crucified Jesus, and their intent was evil; however, it all happened according to God's plan.

It seems that no matter what humans intend by their actions, what God planned is what will happen. God's reasons for what he makes happen are known only to Him. Theologians have called this concept the "sovereignty of God." No Christian group owns it; it cuts across denominational lines. Augustine, Bishop in Hippo, North Africa, believed it. The Roman Catholic Jansenists of the Port Royal Abbey, with whom Pascal was associated, believed it.[32] Luther did, followed by Calvin, who developed the teaching perhaps more than any theologian, making it the hallmark doctrine of Reformed and Presbyterian Churches.

The authors of the seventeenth-century Scottish Presbyterian Confession of Faith expressed it this way: "God from all eternity did, by the most wise and holy counsel of his own will, freely and unchangeably

---

[32] From Cornelius Jansen, a Catholic university professor who died in 1638. Their teaching was similar to Calvinism. The Jansenists were opposed by the Jesuits. The Abbey at Port Royal was considered the center of their theological school.

ordain whatsoever comes to pass." (Chapter 3:1). The rest of the sentence concludes with philosophical caveats.

However, what are the implications of this teaching? That would mean, for example, the Jewish Holocaust in Nazi Germany was the will of God. He determined it would occur and orchestrated all contingencies to ensure it. The attack on the World Trade Center on 9/11 was the will of God in the same way. Crimes and tragedies on a global scale occurred as part of God's mysterious plan, the ends of which are unknown to us. This teaching is believed by millions of evangelicals today. Not all evangelicals embrace this teaching.

Evangelicals who believe in the sovereignty of God don't condone genocides or hate crimes that take millions of lives. While they soundly condemn such atrocities, they nevertheless profess that God ordained they should happen while insisting God is not the author of sin—a conundrum. Why would God ordain such horrible crimes? They will say, "He has a plan. It is a mystery we cannot fathom. We must trust God for what he allows." However, ordaining something to happen and allowing it is incongruous.

I believed in the sovereignty of God for most of my adult life, and I feel ashamed that I did. There are a few dozen or more evangelical denominations that require their ministers to profess they believe it. However, they largely remain quiet about it.

The Will of God and Politics

In January 2019, White House spokesperson Sarah Huckabee Sanders, in an interview on the Christian Broadcasting Network, commented that it is "God's will that Donald Trump was elected president." She said this in response to Nancy Pelosi reportedly saying that building the border wall is immoral. Here's what Sarah said:

> "I think God calls all of us to fill different roles at different times, and I think that he wanted Donald Trump to become president, and that's why he's there. I think he has done a tremendous job in supporting a lot of things that people of faith really care about."

What did she mean? Donald Trump's election was a good thing? For whom? Did God want Trump to become president because he was pleased with him? Is his presidency good for all people of faith— American, Central American, and Mexican, or only citizens of the

United States? What about people of other religions or no faith? Her statement seems to communicate that God chose Donald Trump to become president because he was pleased with him and gave him as a gift to evangelical fundamentalists. They have said that, and that is why he is their president.

Her statement reflects how mixing religion with politics muddies the water of public discourse. They believe inserting religious convictions into public policy is good and determining political discourse apart from faith is wrong. Her statement also reflects the ambiguity associated with the phrase "the will of God" or "plan of God." More disconcerting is that millions of evangelicals in the United States agree with Sarah Sanders.

"It Wasn't God's Will."

The most common circumstance in which Christians use the expression, "it wasn't the will of God," is when faced with an unwanted outcome. For example, if voters do not reelect Donald Trump, "it will not be God's will," regardless of their prayers and votes. God is in control. They never quite seem to grasp the inconsistency of what they are saying. If it is God's plan and he is in control, why vote?

Another example of the expression is when evangelicals offer prayers for God to heal someone of cancer, but if they aren't, it's because "it wasn't God's will." I cannot tell you how many times I heard that comment as a pastor. I stopped using that language because I was beginning to doubt it.

However, evangelicals have a positive way of describing a negative outcome. You may hear, "God answered our prayers, but not in the way we had hoped. He wanted to bring her (the deceased) home" (she died and went to heaven). You can pray for a positive outcome, but if it isn't God's plan, it won't happen. The caveat to prayer is often, "thy will be done. Amen."

Predestination

Evangelical theologians extended the teaching of God's sovereignty to include spiritual salvation. You can find it in Paul's letter to the Romans, Chapters 9-11, and in Ephesians 1:11: "In him we [believers] were also *chosen*, having been *predestined* according to the plan of him who works out everything in conformity with the purpose of his will" (TNIV). The word "predestined" from the Greek is *proorizo*: to *decide beforehand* according to the *plan* (*prothesine*) of him [God] who works out everything in conformity with the purpose of his *will* (*thelamatos*). God chose people who believe for salvation before he created the earth; they are the *elect*.[33] Another way of expressing it is "God chose them to believe." Those who go to hell were not chosen but left to perish as judgment for their sins. John Calvin emphasized predestination in positive terms to avoid *double predestination*: God predestined some to heaven and others to hell.

Those evangelicals who believe in predestination identify themselves as Calvinists, as John Calvin was one of the more notable proponents of this teaching (Institutes of the Christian Religion, Book 3, Chapters 21-24). However, many other Protestant theologians believed in predestination, including Martin Luther, who preceded Calvin by a generation. The final architect of Lutheran theology, however, was Philip Melanchthon, the theologian and Lutheran church leader in the following generation who turned the Church away from the teaching of predestination and emphasized *free will*—God is sovereign in all things, except human salvation. Thomas Cranmer, the first Anglican Archbishop of Canterbury during the reign of King Henry VIII, was a Calvinist, as were many priests in the early Church of England.[34]

The teaching of predestination is embraced today by thousands of Presbyterians, Reformed Church members, some Baptists, and independent evangelicals. More liberal Protestant denominations in the United States no longer subscribe to the teaching. As expected, most Christians and many, if not most, evangelicals have rejected the teaching as repugnant—the dignity of choice and free will must be upheld.

In salvation, however, it is the Holy Spirit who effectuates (produces) salvation in the elect. Calvinists believe while God has predestined individuals to salvation, the Holy Spirit enters the lives of the elect at an appointed time in their lives, especially but not always, when they hear the *Gospel* or recall it. An old friend of mine related how he was *saved* while employed picking onions in California, right there in the field in the middle of the day. The Spirit enables the elect to respond

---

[33] The moniker *elect,* used for the faithful of Yahweh, was used by the author of Enoch (*righteous and elect ones*, 39:8-9). However, it may be used in the sense of *special*.

[34] Articles of Religion of the Church of England, Articles XVII (17), Of Presdestination and Election.

with faith to the gospel message. The beginning of salvation is a combination of the *effectual call* of God with the work of the Spirit. What is at work in the heart of the elect is referred to as *irresistible grace*. An elect person will not resist the Spirit but yield to its gentle and inaudible persuasion. The elect will have a saving epiphany as they are *born again.*

The doctrine of the sovereignty of God and predestination has its conundrums. It is an example of how intellectual imagination can coexist with faith. The primary author of this teaching was the Apostle Paul.

Chapter 15

Faith vs. Science

Knowledge is the pure definition of *science*. Few people know this. When I attended *Philosophy of the Christian Faith* class, two semesters required of all Juniors at Shelton College, I learned Theology is a science, a well-organized cocktail of biblical interpretations, the history of Christian doctrine with a dash of Greek and enlightenment philosophy. It was a tough class. There was a lot of memorization.

We usually think of science as knowledge of the phenomenal world apart from religious teachings or sacred texts. We refer to it as natural science. Perhaps some of the most impactful sciences are botany, biology, medicine, mathematics, physics, aerodynamics, electronics, meteorology, and astronomy. Natural science depends on close observation, experimentation, and demonstration. I'm sure you can detect I'm not a scientist, and I won't pretend to be, but I am a curious learner who appreciates natural science.

Evangelical friends tell me we can't know everything through natural science. They say this when they are defending a six-day creation of the cosmos. They also tell me that scientists are not infallible. I agree with them. Scientists make a lot of mistakes, but they don't claim to be infallible, and they are open to corrections. I find them always correcting themselves or each other, and they are continually improving their hypotheses, making progress, and refining their discoveries. They are getting a lot of things right.

That's how scientists like the Wright brothers figured out how to fly their plane at Kitty Hawk, North Carolina, in 1903. They learned and improved by trial and error—by repeatedly failing, then getting it right. The DC-3 made its first flight only thirty-two years later. In 1957 Soviet scientists sent *Sputnik 1* into outer space. That was rapid aeronautic progress. Medical science has made incredible progress in the last hundred years, even during the previous five years. The development of scientific achievement is exponential.

No. I don't think scientists know everything. They would be the first to admit it. The more scientists learn about their respective fields of study, the more they realize they don't know and the humbler they become. But they learn more and more each month about the real world and apply that knowledge to discoveries that benefit us all. They study the real world, the world about which we can all agree regardless of our religious orientation or irreligiosity.

Science and Imagination

Imagination is essential to science. The Wright brothers imagined the first airplane before they created the prototype. The inventions of Leonardo da Vinci began in his imagination. Some failed while others succeeded. The author Jules Verne envisioned submarines and rockets to the moon in the nineteenth century. Thomas Edison relied on his creativity and determination to find a light bulb filament that wouldn't burn out. Most great scientific discoveries and inventions began with a vision, while others discovered them accidentally.

There is, however, a considerable difference between scientific and religious imagination. Religious imagination is gullible. It requires faith in people who claim God speaks to them with a message for the tribe. They are the prophets who expect the members of the tribe to disregard their observations of the phenomenal world and to believe in the supernatural. The problem with the credibility of the prophet is that no one can vet his communication with the gods. One must suspend his or her doubt and believe. Belief becomes faith and trust. One trusts the prophet and, consequently, the sacred text, the words of the prophets.

The willing suspension of disbelief is essential to the storyteller and her or his audience. There is an agreement between both parties. The storyteller expects people in the audience to suspend their disbelief and imagine the events of the story as entertainment. The people in the audience, regardless of age, participate. Without this agreement, we couldn't enjoy reading fiction or watching movies like *Jaws* or *Star Wars*. We begin to learn the skill as toddlers.

Religion began with storytelling, and the tellers were prophets and shamans. The stories were about the ancestors and messages from the gods for them and their descendants: "This is what the gods say and what the gods expect." The story was also about what the gods did when they were displeased. People believed the prophets and feared the gods. How else could ancient humans have understood the world? They were understandably gullible.

The priests were the authorities and depended on the power of imagination and rhetoric. There was no one to question them; if there was, his or her life was in jeopardy. The quick alliance between priest and chieftain was immediate. Together, they protected and promoted each other and formed the hegemony over the community they intimidated and ruled. Priests were the original propagandists.

Scientific imagination looks for real possibilities without messages from God or divine intervention. The Airbus flies not because God makes it fly but because engineers designed it aerodynamically. Hurricane Michael destroyed Mexico Beach, Florida, not because it was God's plan but because it was a severe weather phenomenon. The hurricane's path was predicted days before using computer models. Devastating as they are, hurricanes are naturally occurring events that strike along the eastern shore of the Atlantic to the Gulf of Mexico. God is not part of the equation.

The Real World

If you understand the books of the Bible the way their authors intended them to be understood, you are adopting an ancient, supernatural interpretation of reality. The world of our ancestors was filled with magic, angels, and demons profoundly affecting people's lives every day. Demons caused physical and mental illness. If that was the cause of disease in Jesus' time, why shouldn't it be now? I have known Christians who believe demons are responsible for disease, especially mental illness. I listened to one of Billy Graham's sermons on YouTube in which he told a large crowd that some cases of mental illness are probably the result of demon possession.

With the passing of the middle ages and the dawn of the seventeenth-century enlightenment, theologians had to adjust their understanding of reality. They recognized the cosmos is ruled by the *laws of nature*—the natural physical laws that govern the universe, discovered by physicists and mathematicians.

The enlightenment was also the beginning of the great rift within Christianity. Those who were won over to the scientific explanation of the world realized the Bible could not be relied upon for scientific truth. It isn't a science textbook. The positive messages in its books are intended to cultivate faith in God, not explain the cosmos. The earth was not created in six literal days; Moses did not part the waters of the Red Sea so the Hebrews could cross on dry ground, nor did the sunshine for

48 hours while Joshua slaughtered his enemies. God didn't command Joshua to kill every man, woman, and child in Jericho (if it happened). Did Jesus really rise from the dead? Is there a way to understand his resurrection metaphorically?

Conservative theologians and clerics were determined to defend the inerrancy and infallibility of the Bible. God inspired its authors, so what they wrote is the *Word of God—what it says about everything is accurate and reliable*. The miracles recorded in Scripture are factual, even though they don't occur today. Of course, many believe in cheap miracles. TV news anchors often refer to a miracle delivering people from an accident or disaster. The lady who survived after a tornado destroyed her home declared it was a miracle, but it killed her neighbor. God is sparing in handing out miracles.

Modern Compromise

Theologians and clerics, who embrace science, choose a more difficult path. They recognize myths and contradictions in the Bible. They excuse the prophets and apostles as bound by the ignorance and prejudice of their time. Jesus may or may not have risen from the dead. It doesn't matter; there are other ways to understand that. Faith in God must be preserved because it fosters a positive social structure. A community of faith and edification should be maintained.

Modernists introduced smorgasbord Christianity. Accept what you like and reject the rest as you see fit. "Dogmatism be damned." Because they couldn't abandon the Bible or rewrite it, they must regard and use it differently. Doctrinal teachings have vanished. The only lessons that matter are positive and compassionate, whether they are found in the Psalms or the words of Jesus. Those are the only things that matter. Many Psalms of David are included. The poetic monologue of the Apostle Paul on love is also acceptable (I Cor. 13). Harsher, vitriolic passages will be ignored.

What's in the Bible will be there forever. Like the Quran, the Book of Mormon, or the Works of Shakespeare, it will always be part of our literary heritage. No one may delete noxious passages, but neither should one use them. As I recognized very early in my ministry, some passages in the Bible are inappropriate readings to a congregation— children are present.

In the new compromise, the divine inspiration of the Bible is difficult to define; let each express his or her interpretation unless it's politically incorrect; in that case, keep it to yourself or suffer the consequences. Political correctness is the new dogmatism.

I can think of one old mainline Protestant denomination that is more broad than liberal. Depending on the congregation, the region, the city, or the country, churches can be very liberal or very conservative.

Evangelical Compromise

Evangelicals who claim to believe the Bible is the inspired and inerrant *Word of God* have arranged a different smorgasbord. The menu calls for keeping the message positive, practical, and constructive while avoiding the darker, negative messages of the Bible. Don't tell people they're going to hell for their sins or their LGBTQ lifestyles. Tell them you love them, and God loves them. Lead them into a relationship with Jesus Christ, and everything will take care of itself.

I recently watched the interview of an evangelical pastor who changed his perspective on the LGBTQ community. He once taught his congregation that an LGBTQ lifestyle is sinful, requiring the sinner's repentance. He saw the error of his ways and changed his mind. He and the congregation accept them as they are and expect no change in their lifestyles. They moved comfortably into the twenty-first century. However, doing so requires adjustments in how they understand and use the Bible. The Old Testament condemns homosexuality (Leviticus 18:22). The Apostle Paul condemned homosexuality and lesbianism as recorded in Romans 1:24-27. Regardless of how the church determines to disregard biblical directives, evangelicals who don't adopt twenty-first-century values will only highlight their backwater fundamentalism.

Religion evolves at a very fast rate.

Chapter 16

Healing and Freedom

In July 2008, I announced to my congregation that I would resign at the end of the year. I also resigned from the denomination to which I belonged. Resignation accepted, I declared myself an independent minister. I had been ordained by a group of independent pastors 28 years earlier. I considered developing an independent ministry, but at the same time, I began to question what I had been taught about the Bible. I had been questioning parts of it for a while as a pastor.

While some lessons in the Bible would continue to support my values, others could not. As if drawing a veil from my eyes, I began to see the Hebrew Bible and the New Testament for what they are—human documents about the religious beliefs of ancient peoples.

After my resignation, the personality I buried at age 19 reemerged. I happily greeted the person I once was—the humanist. I thought, *"What am I going to do with my life?"* After a few failed attempts at employment, I got my license to sell health and life insurance. Though it is only an occupation, I have been content with it. However, a livelihood is never enough to fill a life.

I started thinking about the Bible and religious faith—what I believed and what I didn't, what is true and what isn't. I realized the Bible contained myth, exaggeration, and contradictions. I began reading modern works by biblical scholars who wrote for the general public instead of scholarly colleagues. (Books on biblical criticism can be very long, technical, and tedious. I read some of them). I understood what they were saying about the Bible.

Rabbis and scribes, then priests and monks, edited the biblical texts. The same clerics decided which books were in and which were out until they completed the Canons of both. Despite what synagogues and churches teach, it is not the inspired, inerrant Word of God. It doesn't reveal God's will for human beings. The image of God we form from its pages is super-human, but human still. I no longer need to quench a spiritual thirst with divine water. The water of life is to enjoy each day as a gift from the universe.

I didn't note when it happened, but somewhere in the middle of my 60th year, I let go of my faith in God. I guess that makes me an atheist—a noxious title in the opinion of some. I don't like titles, but I suppose we must live with them. I no longer believe in a god with a personality, infinite knowledge, and unlimited power. He, she, or it doesn't exist, doesn't have to exist. There is no heaven. There is no hell. There is only the cosmos, and we live in it. If anything is my god, it is the cosmos. It makes no demand. It issues no threats.

I experienced a great deal of relief. It was a less cathartic epiphany. I trusted my mind, reflections, and conclusions. I didn't have to answer to anyone. I have only to respect my neighbor and the laws of the nation and state in which I live, even if I don't believe in all of them. If I break them, I will have to answer to a judge. I don't need an authority higher than that. I have the sense of right and wrong my parents instilled in me without any reference to the Bible or religion. They taught me by example, especially by the way they treated other people. They were far from perfect, they weren't rich, but I was lucky to be born to them.

Did the Bible contribute to the innate sense of right and wrong? Of course, it did. So did every piece of literature ever written—poetry, fiction, and non-fiction—to heighten the human sensibilities of love, kindness, compassion, respect, and peace. As humans, we created those sensibilities as we evolved. We cannot prosper without them.

The oldest religious texts depict a god who is angry, jealous, vengeful, and brutal. As we progressed, the image of god evolved with us. The classical Hebrew prophets increasingly described a god who is merciful and compassionate. Though the beliefs, ignorance, and prejudices of his time hampered Jesus, many portrayals of him describe a sensitive man who had compassion for the poor and suffering. The New Testament reveals different portraits of Jesus. Was he a man of peace, or a wrathful god-man who slaughters his enemies? Was Jesus conflicted? Probably. The writers of the books in the New Testament and the people who collected those books were the ones who were conflicted. The same conflict has dogged Christianity to this day.

Religion evolves with our sensibilities, much faster than we evolve physiologically. Progress never stops. It only gets interrupted but always resumes.

Caution

Religious fundamentalism, in whatever religion, results in a cultic following, and cult followers become tools in the hands of cult leaders and demagogues. Cults are not restricted to religion. Toxic religious and non-religious ideologies attract cult followers today. Political leaders attract cult followers.

You don't need to follow anyone. Think for yourself and question everything.

CPSIA information can be obtained
at www.ICGtesting.com
Printed in the USA
BVHW031004150321
602551BV00012B/665/J

9 781087 954059